COWPHOON

COWPHOON

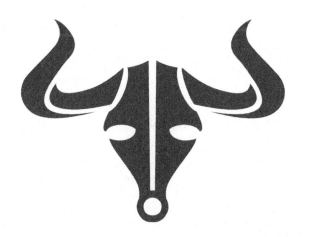

GLEN W. GRANHOLM

Cover Design: Larry Blamire

Interior Design: Slaven Kovaevi

Editor: Liz Cole

Wagyu Press Books

ISBN-13: 978-0-9989631-0-5

This book is a work of fiction. Names, places, characters, events and incidences used and described are the product of the author's imagination and any resemblance to person or persons living or dead, or events or places is entirely coincidental. Except for the Cow Palace. That really is a place. I've been there.

With Deepest Thanks:

To Trish:
For everything, including
"Keep It Stupid and Keep It Coming."

To Chuck:
Who thought muumuus
could be so funny?

To Ravyn:
For timely cow humor and telling me
I just wasn't trying.

Cowphoon would not have been possible
without the amazing assistance of:

Larry Blamire: What a cover! Boy was I wrong
when I thought skeletons
were the only things in your
wheelhouse.

Liz Cole: Editor extraordinaire-your
detailed direction kept me on
track and the cows in order.

PROLOGUE

Wagyu Island is, most often, hidden in the mist. A nearly continual band of fog hides the island from view of the north shore of the Oriental mainland so that few people know of the cay's existence. Even fewer venture the mile and a half out – be it on raft, canoe or dinghy – to visit the densely vegetated isle. Sharp, angry, black rocks surround most of the shoreline so that, even if one could make it across the often choppy waters and unpredictable current separating Wagyu from the mainland proper, one would be hard-pressed to find a place to moor one's raft, canoe or dinghy. So isolated was Wagyu.

Yet, isolation rarely means the same thing as uninhabited, and uninhabited Wagyu was not. At least, not before what came to be called "The Incident." Buried deep within the overgrowth, down a crooked and nearly invisible path on the Pacific side of Wagyu, was a building teeming with scientific activity. The nondescript steel structure was about the size of any modern roast beef fast food restaurant and was surrounded by a six-foot-tall fence. An electrified fence. A small metal sign hung at eye level (to a five-foot scientist) on the only entry door to the building. The sign simply said: Yonezawa Research.

Anyone checking into Yonezawa Research would discover that it was a company that studied the many properties of oleaginous fat and its effect on intense marbling. But that description was simply a clever ruse put in place years before to deter anyone who had happened to stumble out to the island, anchor their craft and make their way through the dense foliage (the creatures of which are highlighted in another story), past the electrified fence and up to the door of the place. One might see the sign on the door, do a quick smartphone search (though cell signal on Wagyu was iffy at best) and say, "Oleaginous fat research? I should have guessed. Nothing to see here." Then they would simply turn back.

Clearly the sign had performed its duties splendidly, as nobody had ever tried to gain entry into the building in the fifteen years Dr. Yan Mishima had been on the island. His trusted assistant, Matt Susaka (called "Matt-san" by Dr. Mishima), would run excursions to the Oriental mainland to get the provisions and scientific implements needed for the top-secret research that was, in reality, taking place on Wagyu. No, there were no oleaginous fat studies going on here. Not by a long shot. Not even close.

Matt, now laden with assorted capacitors and needle scopes, stood at the ready, offering up an array of devices for Dr. Mishima.

"Is one of these what you are looking for, Professor Stan?" queried Matt-san, hoping to have got it right this time.

"No, no, Matt-san," replied Dr. Mishima. "I asked for a paper towel. And please, call me Dr. Mishima. How many times must I request that of you?"

"Oh, sorry. A paper towel you say? Do we have those?"

Matt Susaka was, in the mind of Dr. Mishima, a perfect example of the old adage "Good help is hard to find." The doctor was sure that phrase originated in the Bible somewhere. *"Probably Pharaoh said it,"* he thought.

Still, despite his obvious shortcomings, Matt-san was dear to the scientist. The faithful Matt-san had stayed on longer than any other assistant, even sticking around after the now-infamous "Whack-a-Mole Experiment," and anyone resilient enough not to throw in the towel (another Biblical phrase?) after that would, in Dr. Mishima's mind, have a position as trusted lab assistant for life.

Now, all musings aside, throw in the towel was exactly what Dr. Mishima wanted Matt to do. The scientist had just spilled his coffee.

"Try the kitchen, Matt-san. There are usually paper towels there."

The good doctor and dedicated helper were on the verge of a truly historic scientific breakthrough: the miniaturization of nuclear power. Once a fanciful idea bandied about over countless evenings of saké and hacky sack, the Nucliette, as it affectionately came to be named, was about to become functional. It represented the first truly new method of producing power since the last scientific breakthrough in the field.

Where is that kid?" Dr. Mishima wondered, dabbing at the spilled coffee on the black workbench, using his lab coat sleeve because Matt-san hadn't returned from the kitchen. He stared for the umpteenth time at the glowing box an arm's length away.

The Nucliette was about the size of a model 99763 compact refrigerator. It resembled a purple, oblong cube. In fact, Matt-san often referred to it as "the purple, oblong cube." It had a door that could swing open like that of a toaster oven, or even a large oven. The insides of the Nucliette consisted of some highly radioactive elements, so it was always best to leave the door to the unit closed. In fact, it was the problem of the pesky radioactivity leakage that was keeping the doctor from launching the unit commercially on a worldwide scale. Dr. Mishima reasoned that, if he could create a door that could allow access while safely containing the radiation, it might also increase the Nucliette's efficiency.

And then, in an instant, he had it! Dr. Mishima had the answer he'd been searching for all these untold years. *"It sounds crazy, I know it does,"* thought the professor.

"No, it would never work," he responded to himself, now perilously close to an internal conversation that might, for all intents and purposes, never end.

"What won't work, Dr. Fonz?" asked Matt-san.

Three things were immediately clear to Dr. Mishima. Firstly, his internal "it would never work" response to his internal "it sounds crazy" comment was not just internal, it was external. Secondly, Matt-san had clearly gotten something mixed up on his mission to get the paper towels. He stood there holding a toilet plunger. And lastly, it was quite likely Matt-san would never get Dr. Mishima's name right.

Dr. Mishima sighed. "I have an idea to fix the issue of the leaking radioactivity on the Nucliette, but now I am doubting such a radical idea will work at all."

"The what?" asked Matt-san.

"The Nucliette," replied Dr. Mishima, pointing at the compact refrigerator-sized box.

"Oh, you mean the purple, oblong cube? Why don't you just not put a door on it, Dr. Ron?"

That was exactly the thought Dr. Mishima had in mind, and for years afterward the good doctor would chastise himself for not having thought of it sooner. So absorbed were he and Matt-san in the discussion of the door that Mishima didn't notice the rumbling sound that was coming from outside the research building. The din of the lab processing equipment masked the sound at first, but gradually the noise got louder. When the nuclear entrepreneur finally realized something bad was about to happen, a forty-foot wall of water smashed into the side of the building. The giant wave crashed into the lab, tossing everything every which way, including the doctor and his somewhat capable assistant. Years' worth of scientific research was destroyed in moments and, though the two men survived the sudden rush of water in one piece, the Nucliette was not so lucky. Within minutes, the purple, oblong cube was headed out to sea. It was only after the scientist and his assistant were safe again on dry land that the doctor noticed Matt-san was holding the door of the Nucliette in his right hand. He'd grabbed it from the swirling water during the sudden flood. He thought it was the paper towels.

PART ONE:

LIKE SO MUCH FLOTSAM

O NLY ONE PERSON HAS EVER attempted to get a degree in meteorolonomics – the study of the impact of weather on the economy. The intense combination of science, mathematics and sociology may lead one to believe that it is too difficult, but the fact of the matter is, no school had ever thought to combine the seemingly incongruous study arenas into one cohesive unit. That is, until Dean Kuri Malvi introduced the major into the bachelor's program options at Aberdeen Angus University in the mid–seventies. The dean's hope was that offering up some clever majors such as meteorolonomics would attract some out–of–state students whose higher tuition rates would help bolster the college's sagging bottom line. But, unfortunately for all concerned, nobody was lured by the opportunity to become the world's first meteorolonomicist while Dean Malvi presided, as intriguing as that possibility sounded. He was decades-retired before the first student ever tried earning a degree in the field.

Devon Steerman was that first student. And now, smack dab in the middle of studying the latest West Coast weather maps overlaid atop a recent issue of the *Stock Street Journal*, the young man paused to ponder the events that had led him down the path to his cubicle in the basement of the Floral and Dance Sciences building at Aberdeen Angus University, or AAU as the locals called it. Raised on a small dairy farm located just a few miles away from the campus, Devon was nerdy, bright and amiable; a tall and lanky type, who often reminded people of a rather intelligent puppy. His mom had left to join the circus (or so Devon was told) when he was just a few months old, and so the task of raising the boy was left to his father, John. And though it may have seemed impossible for him to leave father and farm behind, once high school was completed Devon didn't have to think twice about heading to the bright lights and big city up Highway One to attend AAU. Of course, John couldn't afford to send his son off to college – no dairy farmer could – and if it wasn't for the full-ride scholarship Devon had earned with his essay on beef lips, college would have been out of the question.

Choosing meteorolonomics as a major, though now the obvious choice for Devon, almost didn't happen. At the beginning of his sophomore year he was volunteering at a recycling drive at the Ala Tau fraternity. He was stacking bundles of old newspapers tied up with twine in the back of a van when a faded issue dropped to the ground. It looked quite old and, as it turned out, it was a copy of the AAU campus newspaper, *The Lampurger*, from the late seventies. Intrigued, Devon flipped through the pages to see what the current events were back then. Apparently, the men's synchronized limbo team was doing well. The mayor's annual lawn fork competition was in a few days. A review of the previous week's Stinky Hooves concert at the AAU auditorium indicated the event was a definite hit. And there, just between the column on using motor oil to cook French fries and the article on Tabby Cat Awareness Week, was a story that caught Devon's eye. It was titled, "Who Gnu? AAU's Proprietary Fields of Study." And that one article changed Devon's life, forever.

For years, Belmont "Red" Simford was the country's most successful Tauros car dealer. He owned an oversized car dealership, covering more than forty acres just outside of Dexter. In fact, Red was the epitome of the popular saying "Everything's bigger in Dexter" because everything about Red was oversized. He lived in an oversized house, more than fifty thousand square feet, laid out on his oversized ranch located adjacent to the Deep Red River. He had an oversized wife, oversized kids and wore an oversized, twenty-gallon hat that went well with his dark, deep-set eyes and oversized handlebar mustache. He drove the largest Tauros ever built: a three-row, nine-seat, twenty-foot-long beast, complete with giant steer horns mounted across the front, custom-built for him to drive about his car lot, greeting potential buyers with a bellowed "Howdy." Recently, Simford's sales totals had been surpassed by an upstart, non-oversized dealer out on the West Coast. And, while this dealer was technically no competition at all to Red and Simford Auto Sales, Red simply could not stand the thought of being second-best at anything. He claimed he never could, and never would.

Ever since Tauros' parent company had released national sales figures to all dealers weeks earlier, Red had begun planning to knock the new number one dealership out of that position and reclaim his place at the top of the heap. That's where Simford's had sat since the brand made its infamous entry into the coupe convertible crossover sedan market and Red's pappy had started selling Tauros RX3 Coupes, some thirty years back. Red's idea was to hold a car sale extravaganza south of the city out west, and capture just enough regional sales to cut into the totals being brought in by the local and new number one dealer.

Many strategizing sessions had already occurred, and Red had called another meeting of his Brain Trusters, as he liked to refer to them, because one of his employees, Dutch Friesian, had texted Red that he had some big news. When the Brain Trusters had finally gathered around the oversized picnic table next to the dealership's combination putting green and laundromat, Red started the meeting with his usual, no-nonsense approach.

"Well, Dutch, what's the big news?"

Dutch Friesian looked about as weasel-like as anyone had ever looked. He had short black hair, small ears, sharp, pointed teeth and eyes that continually darted about whenever he was in the company of other people. He hesitated a bit too long before answering Red's question.

"C'mon, ya weasel, out with it. What's the big news ya tixted me about?"

Red never could get the lingo right when it came to modern electronics, or most other modern things.

Dutch's eyes dashed about the table, from fellow Brain Trusters Murray Grey to Parda Alpina, then Speckle Park and then quickly back to Red. "I got it boss. I got the place."

"Dad-gurnit, Dutch. What the heck are you mutterin' about?"

"I got the place, boss," repeated Dutch.

"What place would that be, ya idjit?" Red bellowed, his thin patience wearing thinner.

"The place for the car sale out west." Dutch grinned, his spiky teeth glinting in the afternoon sun. "I found the perfect place for the car sale. We can have a grand opening and then rent the place for two weeks, long enough to knock Upstart Motors, or whatever they're called, right on their derriere."

Red stood up so that everyone in attendance could easily see his please countenance.

"Well, dang, that is fantastic! Just fantastic."

He let out an oversized, almost maniacal belly laugh. It went on for an uncomfortable amount of time. Then, in mid-guffaw, he suddenly stopped and bent over to plant his fists on the picnic table. His eyes narrowed and he glared from Brain Truster to Brain Truster. He stared at them for another uncomfortable amount of time, saying nothing. Just staring. It took a distant caw from a roaming crow to bring him out of his apparent trance.

Red stood tall again and shouted, "Don't just sit there, get a move on! We've got to get thirty dozen cars out to the West Coast and I mean PRONTO!"

Various Brain Trusters scrambled to get away from the picnic table – not an easy task to accomplish in a hurry – and went scattering off in all directions, except for Dutch, who couldn't move because Red had ahold of him by his shirt collar.

"Not you, Dutch, not so fast," Red fairly whispered into the weasel's ear.

Dutch's eyes darted from the picnic table to the laundromat to a nearby Tauros station wagon and then back to the picnic table.

Red continued, in a voice so faint Dutch had to strain to hear it above his own pounding heart. "You did good, real good, in finding us a spot out west. Ya know, I am going to need a second-in-command to run my West Coast operation, and I'm thinking you'd be perfect for the job."

"I would?" Dutch squeaked, shivering sort of like a frigid Chihuahua. He caught himself and cleared his throat. "Ahem, I mean I would indeed."

Dutch had never thought of himself as a second-in-command kind of guy before. He'd originally been hired to clean up after the elephant rides and occasionally make tea for the Charbray sisters whenever they were in the market for a new Tauros. He reasoned he'd been chosen as a part of the Brain Truster team because of his tea-making ability. He'd never seen an elephant at any of their meetings. He had stumbled upon the location for Red's western car sale because he'd mentioned to a cousin that he was looking for somewhere in the Bay City area to sell cars and his cousin recommended a place where he had just attended a reptile, gun and hemp show. Dutch then called the location and the nice lady on the phone had told him that they'd just had a cancellation so, once the next weekend's combination adult expo, rock and gem conference, and toy train convention were over, the place was un-booked for a couple of weeks.

"Yes, you would indeed." Red smiled and relaxed his grip on the little man's collar. "In fact, I think it's time I stopped calling you The Weasel, my little buddy."

"It is?" Dutch croaked this time, still shaking, and adding, "You call me that?"

"Certainly. From now on I am going to call you The Henchman. It has a nice ring to it, I think, particularly since it is a henchman that is required if we are going to get that no-good West-Coaster out of the top sales spot."

"Okay?"

"So, tell me, The Henchman." Red stopped and laughed, this time for a short and not uncomfortable duration. "What's the name of this place we're going to sell cars out west?

"The place?" asked the newly dubbed The Henchman, his eyes beginning to dart again, now glancing at a nearby trashcan.

"Yes, what is the name of the place? The place at which we will sell cars?" asked Red.

The Henchman answered, "Well, it's called the Cow Palace."

Red released the shaking man's collar. "The Cow Palace... It's perfect!

Contented. That was the way most folks felt whenever they visited John Steerman's little farm. Sure, the farm's name, Contented Corners, had something to do with that. But, regardless of the name, once people passed through the gate and down the tree-lined driveway and back into the tiny hideaway, with its sweet scent of flowers and soothing sound of clucking chickens and running water, they seemed to universally sigh, with a long and relaxed, "Ahhh." Troubles just seemed to melt away at Contented Corners Farm; there was just no way to avoid it.

The farm, located down Highway One, just a few miles from hectic Bay City, seemed like a world away from any and all big city hustle and bustle. Contented Corners had been in the Steerman family since the Gold Rush. John's great-great grandfather, Zubron Steerman, was from Yanbia and had bought and cultivated the land, creating Contented Corners primarily to provide food, clothing and lumber to the small community of fellow Yanbian immigrants who had gathered at the southern tip of Bay City, most of whom were giving it a go in the burgeoning Bay City chicken coop manufacturing industry. Sadly, the West Coast's horrible olive tree blight of the 1880s killed off most of the trees in the region, making it nearly impossible for the Yanbians in the area to find the olive shampoo they required for their annual trick-knee festival, so most of them moved back to their homeland. Zubron stuck it out and, though he had to shut down the lumber mill, he found he could still support his wife and thirty-two children by selling dairy products to other folks up in Bay City. The cows seemed so at ease he originally named the place Contented Cow Corners, but later it was agreed that the cows didn't have exclusivity to that particular feeling at that particular place, and "cow" was dropped from the name.

These days, John and his ranch hand, Caceres, just kept the place looking pristine. John had shut down dairy operations once he was convinced his only son, Devon, had no interest in continuing in the family line of work. The mortgage had long since been paid off, and John had only kept the dairy running in regards to Devon's future. But now that the boy was off getting a college education at AAU, there was just no sense in keeping the business side of Contented Corners operational.

That's not to say there wasn't plenty to do. Caceres had quite the green thumb, and though he spoke little English, the Andalusian transplant knew the farm plant bible, Father Smith's Earth News Guide, forwards and backwards, and was particularly adept at timing the blooms of the various annuals, semi-annuals, biennials and millennials that exploded in color throughout the year. So adept, in fact, that people came from a mile around just to look at the pretty flowers continually in bloom at Contented Corners. The plants he grew had vibrant and gigantic blossoms, buoyed to beauty in most part because of the immigrant's homemade fertilizer. He kept his secret ingredients on a rolling cart inside the barn, and would combine them in a specific order with premeasured amounts of manure from the pile that was set back at the far edge of Contented Corners. Several of Caceres' flowers had won awards at fairs throughout the state, most notably his White Lamphuns with their cinnamon aroma and the incredible Red Polled Ostland blooms, which stood about seven feet tall.

John kept busy in the bucolic setting, caring for the assorted chickens and aardvarks that roamed the grounds of the farm. He also paid special attention to the tiny group of cows still left from the days of the dairy. There was one male, a bull named Beefmaster (or Beefy, as John liked to call him), and five cows. One of the cows had given birth to three adorable calves earlier in the year, and John spent a lot of the time these days rounding up these little ones. On any given day, one calf could be found wandering down by the gate, and another messing around with the aardvarks, both potentially dangerous situations for the young 'uns.

Caceres and John shared the small farmhouse tucked in near the pond and waterfall next to the old oak tree. The house was over one hundred years old, quaint and cozy and suited John just fine. In his early sixties, John was short and still quite strong, with farm-honed muscles and a grip that could crush a walnut. He was a real cowboy-type person, time-transplanted to this century, a man of simple dress and few words. He rarely wore a hat, but whenever women or other visitors would pass him by as he whittled away, seated on the bench on the porch of the old farmhouse, he'd dip his head a bit and raise his hand up as if to touch the brim of a hat, and say politely, "Ma'am." Some folks, particularly male visitors, would find the greeting more than a bit disconcerting. John also liked to reply, "Can't complain," whenever anyone asked him how he was doing, or even sometimes when they didn't, another example of him being a true cowboy-type person.

Another even smaller house, more of a shack really, was located across the pond from John's residence. The old, tiny and hard-of-hearing Margaret O'Leary lived there. Many decades earlier, Mrs. O'Leary had been John's first grade teacher, known then as Miss Randall. Once John's wife had left him to join the circus, Margaret had offered to move into the shack and help care for John's boy. John had always considered the act one of selfless kindness from the wonderful, motherly lady – all rumors of her needing to change her name and escape the law because of some sort of bank robbery notwithstanding.

On one particularly sunny Saturday, as John was carrying one of the calves back up to its mother after having pulled it out of the jelly press, he passed by the O'Leary shack just as the woman was shuffling out the front door.

"John, I was just coming to see you," Margaret said.

John lifted the calf up in his strong right arm so the fingers of his hand could touch his imaginary hat.

"Ma'am," he replied.

"What?" she queried, clearly not hearing his greeting.

"Can't complain," John continued.

"What's that, John?" Mrs. O'Leary responded.

The conversation sort of stalled at that moment. The calf squirmed in John's arms. The movement seemed to inspire Mrs. O'Leary.

"Oh, that reminds me, John. I'm glad you are here. I was coming to tell you. There is a storm coming, John. A big storm, a bad storm. My goiter always acts up when a storm is brewing. And it has never acted up like it acted up this morning. I'm telling you John, it's never been this bad."

John Steerman looked up into the bright blue sky, and then back to Mrs. O'Leary. He again raised the calf, now squirming quite a lot in his ironclad grip, and again touched his imaginary hat.

"Ma'am," he said, and abruptly turned and continued his trek toward the back of the main house and the big red barn.

Mrs. O'Leary watched him head away until a nearby scurrying aardvark caught her attention.

"What?" she asked.

Ꮼ Ꮼ Ꮼ

The shops that lined Lineback Street, from Canchim Tower north to where the street dropped suddenly into its infamous switchbacks, were all quaint. Most of the merchants who ran the shops had lived in the neighborhood for decades, long before the rich yuppie-types had moved in. But the rich yuppie-types had money to spend and the merchants found that, once you got past their unusual garb and sometimes off-putting attitude, the yuppies were truly great customers. Their incursion into the neighborhood had proved beneficial to all, and the merchants' bitterness about what seemed to be the regional forced deportation of the Kurgan people who had originally settled and shared the place with the merchants was mostly dissipated. Not entirely, but mostly. Some of the merchants were still a bit bitter.

Yet the sporadic bitterness did nothing to impact the quaintness of the four-block shopping district, much to the delight of Police Officer Deputy Chris Holstein, who daily patrolled the neighborhood, keeping both rich yuppie shoppers and merchants safe and sound. Officer Holstein was one of a dying breed, a beat cop who walked his assigned territory on his own two feet. The patrol car-less man was a fixture on Lineback Street, in an area of Bay City called Mashona Town after an old Kurgan word meaning "quaint."

Of all the shops along the tree-lined boulevard, Officer Holstein like the china shop the best. He was fascinated with anything to do with the Orient. The actual name of the store was A China Shop and, though Officer Holstein had never actually set foot in the place, he imagined it a store that sold maps of Mongolia, perhaps pieces of wall and maybe even fortune cookies. The front window display, though changed frequently, always showcased an array of dishes, plates, platters, coffee cups and the like, and that confused Officer Holstein from time to time, whenever he thought about it. Had he run the store, he'd thought more than once, he'd at least put wall pieces or maybe a tiger in the window. That, he reckoned, would get people's attention.

But most of the time Officer Holstein didn't think about the display window of A China Shop, and that was because he was a dedicated police officer. And, whether he was needed at the tall Canchim Tower, with its rooftop observation platform and spectacular view of both Bay City and the bay itself, or down at the switchback end of Lineback Street, Officer Chris Holstein could be counted on to be there. Mashona Town was relatively crime-free, and the good people, bitter merchants and rich yuppies alike, had Holstein to thank for that.

On this particular day, around the same time that Mrs. O'Leary was telling John Steerman about her goiter acting up, Officer Holstein received a call on his two-way. It was headquarters. The policeman was, as it happened, across the street from A China Shop, investigating a complaint of a tree root lifting up a sidewalk section and answered the two-way in his typical prompt and overly polite manner.

"Good morning, Officer Holstein here. How are you today?"

"Please respond. Three-oh-two in progress. See the man. Canchim Tower. Press one-one if you copy."

The Bay City Police Department had transitioned to an automated dispatch system two years earlier. Officer Holstein still wasn't used to it.

"Well, I would be more than happy to head down to Canchim Tower and see what is up," the officer replied in an almost sing-song way. He wasn't sure if he remembered what a 302 was; it had been so long since one had been reported. Heck, it had been more than a month since he'd received any call from dispatch.

The automated system responded. "I repeat. Three-oh-two in progress. See the man. Canchim Tower. Press one-one if you copy."

Officer Holstein paused a moment and tried to remember. A 302 either meant a puppy was stuck in a mailbox or a politician had just had his or her dentures stolen. *"Which one is it, I wonder?"* he pondered.

"I repeat. Press one-one if you copy," said the officer's radio.

"Oh, my apologies. I copy, I copy!" Officer Holstein fumbled with his hand-held for a few seconds, frantically pressing buttons. A bit flustered, he eventually pressed the "one" key twice.

"Instructions confirmed," squawked the radio. "Thank you for responding."

A few minutes later, Officer Holstein was standing at the base of Canchim Tower. It wasn't hard to determine who "the man" was from his dispatch instructions, as a plump and pale middle-aged woman in a bright lavender and chartreuse dress hobbled down the front steps of the tower and up to the officer. Holstein knew immediately who she was. The lady was Ivory Chateaubriand, one of the rich yuppies. She had moved to the neighborhood some five years earlier and Officer Holstein had seen her many times in the quaint establishments along Lineback. He'd even seen her coming out of A China Shop a time or two.

Immediately the detective part of Officer Holstein, though dormant for some time, sprang into action. As far as he knew, this woman held no political office. That left only one possible problem for the officer to address.

"Good day to you, Mrs. Chateaubriand," Officer Holstein said happily with a large and theatrical bow. "Now, let's get your puppy out of that mailbox."

Ivory Chateaubriand was clearly taken aback, which the officer mistakenly assumed was because she must have thought he had some sort of psychic power. She did not think this.

"What puppy?" she asked. And before he could respond, she continued, "You've got to come and take a look at this, Officer Holstein. I went up to the observation platform to perform my weekly yoga and yogurt ceremony when I saw the most unusual thing floating out in the ocean." Then she repeated, "You've got to see this. I have no idea what to make of it."

The woman waved for the policeman to follow. She turned and headed through the front doors of the tower, where the spiral staircase led to the top of the building.

Officer Holstein followed along, more than a bit confused. He thought to himself, *"Why in the world would anyone put a mailbox on the top of a tower?"*

ᏇᏇᏇ

The giant wave that decimated Wagyu Island and the Yonezawa Research Center caused devastation throughout the region. And while only a handful of people even knew of the fast-food roast beef restaurant-sized structure, and even fewer knew of the actual science that had been going on there, people all over the world mourned the destruction of some of the truly wondrous places on the planet.

Gone was the amazing Bathtub Plantation of Achham. Gone were the Upside-Down Arches of Akaushi. And, perhaps most disturbing, gone was the beloved September Mansion of the revered and honorable Feets Fjäll and its world-renowned and amazingly odorous Hirsute Skunk Cabbage Garden. Yes, the freak wave of unknown origin, which came to be known as simply "The Incident," was a killer. A killer of people, a killer of mansions and a killer of a lot more. And yet, unbeknownst to all, the killing was just getting started.

For swept away from both the research center and adjacent mainland on that awful and eventful day was a mismatched assortment of wreckage that glommed together into a debris pile of death: a twelve-foot-long knitted mitten, baling wire from some random kindergarten schoolyard and other odds and ends, including random signs, metal doors and terrariums, all bound together into a cohesive and bizarre heap. As tide and time would have it, the debris pile floated west, making its way across the gigantic Pacific Ocean. And in the middle of the bobbing blob, attached firmly to several rolls of orange-flavored flypaper, sat the ominous glowing Nucliette, its front door missing, high-intensity radiation gushing out.

The Pacific glan catfish is a rare and curious species. Sometimes called "loner fish" by native peoples throughout Oceania because they are never seen traveling in schools, and dubbed "explorer fish" by trawler crewmen because of their freakish information-gathering behavior around fishing boats, the Pacific glan catfish is quite a bit of both: loner and explorer.

One small teenaged glan found itself in what is often called the wrong place at the wrong time on a particular mid-summer evening. On an excursion near the surface of the middle-Pacific, somewhere in the vicinity of a gyre, the fish found itself smack dab adjacent to the purple, oblong cube and its cocoon of flotsam. Instinctively drawn to sea junk, the catfish quickly got within a few feet of the pile and was stunned into unconsciousness by the massive radiation leakage. And then, in just a few seconds, the fish began to mutate.

Purplish radiation bathed the previously curious catfish, and its molecules changed quickly and dramatically. Its two-foot body quadrupled in size. It bloated out into a spherical shape, the dorsal fin distorting into something that can only be described as a multi-function tool. It was chock-full of assorted implements: screwdrivers (Phillips and flat-head), a corkscrew, wire cutters and toenail clippers. Its barbels were now elongated, somehow melding with the baling wire from the pile and morphing into twin épée blades. And the eyes, oh those eyes. They changed into something simply too disgusting to describe.

Once the transmutation had occurred, the former Pacific glan catfish sprang suddenly back to life, warped, in effect, by its own curiosity. It was curious no more. Within its small, albeit larger than before, radioactive brain, the instinct to search things out had been replaced by another instinct: the instinct for killing and blood and gore. And, somewhere in that anomalous brain came this message, via whatever method radioactively mutated fish brains transmit messages: *MUST HAVE WHALE.*

And off the creature swam, driven to find some gigantic, mammalian prey. All the while the debris pile floated ever westward.

⊻⊻ ⊻⊻ ⊻⊻

Advanced Gnu Studies was just one of the unique, and for the most part unknown, bachelor's degrees Aberdeen Angus University offered up, Devon learned upon reading the faded article in the old campus newspaper he'd stumbled upon. To say that piqued his interest would be a vast understatement. Devon had been vacillating between earning a degree in either Swiss languages or ancient biology. He knew he had to make that decision soon since he was no longer a freshman and needed to get serious about the direction his education, and to a greater degree his entire life, would go.

But in his mind, the article expanded his options far beyond just these two relatively benign and safe study fields, and opened up a wide array of possible majors to consider. Sure, as the article's title so clearly indicated, he could delve deep into the analysis of all things gnu. There were many other possibilities as well, avenues of education that, as far as Devon could tell, were only available at AAU. The young man could go into research on the history of fish deities with a degree in ichtheotheology, or perhaps study Middle Eastern ancient machinery, where a degree in archeo-Mesopotamian mechanics would fit the bill. Moolinguistics was offered up, the advanced study not of cow speech (as most people thought) but of cow markings and the lost language that may exist in interpreting them. Looking to the future, rather than the past, was also a possible fulfilling study arena for Devon, and AAU featured a fascinating degree in golf astro-cosmology, or how the golf industry might be changed as man inhabits other worlds. This field was often confused with cosmetology cosmology, a field of study almost entirely pursued by women and men named Chaz, who wished to study the impact of interplanetary travel on the salon industry.

But it was meteorolonomics that ultimately caught the fancy of the bright young man and, though it took some scrambling by university administration to dig out the prerequisite classes and course path needed to earn the degree, eventually Devon found himself well on his way to becoming the first-ever graduate in the field.

Kindly Dr. Rathi Herens, Dean of the School of Cryptic Studies, was assigned as Devon's faculty supervisor. And though Dr. Herens had never heard of meteorolonomics, and was far more interested in the history of Sudoku, he worked closely with Devon to learn, and some might say even develop, the process for overlaying financial planning and weather forecasting sciences into one consistent and scientifically acceptable regimen. Traditional and often fiercely jealous would-be chemists, mathematicians, doctors and CPAs scoffed in unison, often verbally and sometimes physically attacking Devon whenever he spoke about studies that involved the co-examination of the stock market, beef prices and the jet stream. The charts and graphs that typically littered his research cubical were colorful and varied, and usually, if you wanted to find Devon, he'd be half-buried beneath the mountain of clutter, graphing out his predicted changes to both the Dow and the morning dew, usually in reverse order.

On one particular day, just around the time that Mrs. O'Leary was talking to John Steerman about her goiter, and Officer Holstein was following Ivory Chateaubriand up the spiral staircase inside Canchim Tower, Devon Steerman sat bolt upright in his chair, startled erect by his sudden revelation.

He yelled to nobody there, "No, it can't be!"

He paused, rechecked a couple of charts and added some figures for the third time on his massive desktop calculator, just to make sure his math was correct. It was. He quickly dialed up Dr. Herens.

The professor had been sound asleep, a by-product of his daily hot steam meditation routine, and answered the phone groggily. "Yes, Dr. Herens here."

"Dr. Herens. It's me, Devon Steerman. You've got to get down here. Something horrible is about to happen. We've got to warn everybody!" Devon was in a state of hyper-agitation.

Dr. Herens, rapidly returning to a normal state of awareness, tried to calm the young student. "Devon. Easy my boy. Eeeeeeasy. Now just slow down, take a deep breath and tell me what the heck is going on. What are you talking about?"

Devon took an abbreviated deep breath, the best he could muster under the circumstances.

The professor interjected. "Slowly count to ten in your mind, take another breath and explain to me what is happening, Devon."

The young man did as directed, and then dove into the crux of the issue. "Dr. Herens, I was looking into the weekly report on pork bellies and celery stalks from the Farm Animal and Vegetable Commission, like I always do, when I noticed an anomaly. So, as is the protocol, I overlaid the predictions in the report onto a graph of the latest Hinterwald analysis of the Pacific Flow, and there can be no mistaking it. A gigantic storm, and I mean 'gigantic' as in the grandmother of all storms, is headed directly this way. It doesn't show on the typical weather maps those idiots are using in the Meteorology Department, but it will in an hour or so. And by then, it will be too late."

Dr. Herens was stunned, though how much of this stun was from this recent news and how much was from his recent meditative exercise the man could not be certain. Truth be told, Dr. Herens didn't quite understand the nuances involved in the research Devon was doing.

"Devon," the professor asked, "when you say this is bad, how bad is it?"

"It's bad, Dr. Herens. People are going to die, a lot of people. My analysis shows there will be a giant storm surge, part of a hurricane, an enormous hurricane. Like a category seven."

Dr. Herens was not an expert in the weather, but he did know, or at this point thought he knew, a couple of important facts. First, there is no such thing as a category seven hurricane. And, second, he knew, partly from his love of musical theater and partly from his knowledge of common facts, that in Hertford, Hereford, Hampshire and the Pacific Ocean, hurricanes hardly happen. The professor then asked Devon one final, vital question before heading out to see him to check over his calculations.

"Devon, son," he said. "Are you telling me everything?"

"Well, there is one more thing, Professor." Devon replied, "And it's not good news either."

"Then tell me, Devon. What is it?"

"It's the celery stalk futures," Devon replied despondently. "They're about to go into the crapper."

Shocked, Dr. Herens dropped the phone.

ᘐᕽᘐᕽᘐᕽ

For the first time in his life, Dutch Friesian felt cocky. Heck, if things kept going this well, he might just get the notion that he really was The Henchman.

Dozens of brand, spanking new Tauros automobiles had been moved across several states and arranged in tidy rows, like sunbeams, splaying out from the historic Cow Palace, located just east of downtown Bay City. More than several decades old, the concrete arena had, in its heyday, been home to the Bay City United Basketball team and had housed all sorts of spectacular events, from musical acts to daredevil motorcycle performers to three-ring circuses. These days, the building was a bit run-down, but still in high demand and continually in use by assorted traveling conferences, shows and religious conventions, events whose organizers couldn't afford a place like the new and ritzy Amerifax Arena right on the water in the high-rent Marina District of Bay City. So, it was quite fortuitous that there happened to be a gap in the schedule for the Simford Tauros Spectacular Car Show. Even a modest turnout and an end result of selling just thirty or so cars would, in Red Simford's mind, be all that was needed to get his dealership back up to its number one ranking.

The Cow Palace parking lot was huge, an enormous bowl-shaped tract of asphalt that afforded the fledgling The Henchman the opportunity to beef up marketing and create some fun and festive additions to the typical, mundane and often excruciating task of shopping for a new car. Dutch had taken to heart Red's quite pointed admonition to the entire Brain Truster team that they all needed to put forth their best effort, because, to quote Red, "The stakes have never been higher." And while the fact of the matter was Dutch really had done nothing at all to facilitate the actual moving of cars, other than at times to serve up some spectacular tea for the group, the man did know how to, almost intuitively, book places and people. Once the cars were in place and on display at the palatial hub, Dutch got to work booking the cherry to go on top of the car sale sundae. Now Dutch Friesian, The Henchman, was sitting down with Belmont "Red" Simford to tell him some great news surrounding the massive car-selling event.

"Let's get right to it, The Henchman." Red began. "What have you got for me?"

The duo sat down at a picnic table just inside the main entry doors to the Cow Palace.

"Well," Dutch answered, staring at the red and white swirls on the tablecloth. He'd developed a staring technique he could use when seated at picnic tables with Red in order to reduce the weasel-like darting his eyes were prone to. "I think you're going to like this."

Red had to admit, a The Henchman staring at a tablecloth was far preferable to a The Henchman whose beady eyes glanced at nearby transistor radios, flagpoles, pinecones and tabs of butter in rapid succession.

Dutch continued. "First off, since we are at the Cow Palace, I thought it would be a good idea to secure the services of a cow mascot. My first four options were booked solid, but I kept at it. I managed to get ahold of Herbie the Heifer who moos for the Fulani Fruitcakes. They won the Intercontinental Leapfrog League Western Division championship. And that cow is hilarious!"

"That is fantastic, The Henchman!" Red bellowed, his over-sized handlebar mustache quivering. "What else you got?"

"Well, again sticking with the Cow Palace theme, I secured the one and only Salers Salorn, world champion Bullfighter from Spanish Europe. Salers will come dressed in full bull-fighting regalia, take pictures and sign autographs for the kids. I am thinking maybe we could hold a mock bullfight with him and Herbie the Heifer. How does that sound, boss?"

"I'm liking it, really liking it. You've got a real knack for this, kid! Anything else?"

"Yeah, I've got one more." The Henchman continued. He was on a roll and he knew it. "Now, this one doesn't have anything to do with cows, per se. It more has to do with the fact this place is a palace. A palace for cows, but a palace nonetheless."

"Okay... okay... I'm following you so far." Red's curiosity was at a boiling level. "Come on, out with it!"

Dutch continued. "What would you say if I told you I landed the country's most infamous celebrity impersonator, Siri Batangas?"

"I'd say a couple of things," Red responded. "I'd say, 'How in the world did you pull that off?' And then I'd say, 'What does a celebrity impersonator have to do with either selling cars or this place being a palace?'"

"Well, follow my reasoning, boss," The Henchman said. "Siri Batangas impersonates presidents and movie stars and cartoon characters. And all of those are really great. But his pizza resistance, if you will, is his incredible take off on The King."

Red was suddenly and not mildly confused. "What king would that be, The Henchman? King Henry XI? Olav II? Louis XXIII? You've lost me."

Not that Dutch could have guessed, but Red Simford was an expert, not only at the selling of automobiles, but on kings and all things related to them. In fact, in his younger, formative days, Red considered pursuing a college degree in automobile regalological studies, offered up, he'd heard, by some small college out west. The man's skill in selling cars was top notch, but his insight into kings was out of this world.

Red continued. "I mean, are you talking King Midas, a chessboard king, or the infamous and ancient 'Book of Kings?' Which is the 'King' the man so adeptly impersonates? I'd like to know."

Red's impeccable and varied knowledge of kings threw Dutch for a loop. He had to look furtively for things to glance at near the picnic table. There wasn't much to choose from. A fire extinguisher over there. A door hinge over here. A drinking fountain about twenty feet away. Quick, darting looks, a deep breath and a refocusing on the picnic table allowed the somewhat flummoxed The Henchman to continue.

"You know, boss. The King. The King of Rock. This guy has the cape, the neck towel, the 'hunka hunka,' everything! He's perfect. A real showstopper."

Sudden insight came in a flash over the automobile agency owner. Now he understood. This was no literal king to whom The Henchman was referring, but instead a man called "The King." He found the revelation both relieving and disturbing. Red frowned. His eyes narrowed. And then he pulled off his signature move: he put both fists down on top of the picnic table. He looked at The Henchman and began to scowl. Dutch had to think fast, or the whole entertainment plan would come crashing down. He stared hard at the tablecloth.

"I know it's a stretch, boss, but what if we did this? What if we have Siri Batangas bullfight with Herbie the Heifer, or better yet have him put on the mascot outfit and fight Salers Salorn?"

The idea washed over Red like a cool summer rain. His tensed-up body relaxed and an oversized smile erupted across his face.

"Aww, The Henchman, you've done it again. My boy, you've done it again."

It was at that very moment, right around the time that Mrs. O'Leary was telling John Steerman about her goiter, and Officer Holstein was climbing the staircase of Canchim Tower with Ivory Chateaubriand, and Devon Steerman was telling Dr. Herens about his discovery regarding the weather and celery stalk futures, that one of the Brain Trusters, a stocky teenager with a marked propensity for driving manual transmissions, rushed in through the front doors.

Sweaty, agitated, and short of breath, he stammered, "Boss, come quick. You've got to see this!"

Red was out the door in a flash and Dutch found himself banging his knees attempting to get away from a picnic table in rapid fashion. A few seconds later, he too was out the door where he saw Red and several other people gazing up into the eastern sky, down the Bay City Peninsula and out and away toward the Centralized Valley. In an otherwise cloudless blue sky was a cloud formation, maybe two or three hundred feet tall, unlike anything The Henchman had seen before. It looked for all the world like a tornado, swirling madly in the afternoon sky, except for two startling differences. First off, this tornado didn't touch the ground; the whole of it was far above the horizon. And second, the entire funnel cloud was upside down, with the narrow point at the top and the wide section at the bottom. It looked an awful lot like a giant, spinning dunce cap.

"Okay," Red said to everyone gathered. "That's not something you see every day."

Scientists these days, particularly scientists who study the ocean, will argue for hours about whether or not the mammals that live throughout the seven seas are self-aware. Can they think? Can they reason? (Not the scientists, the animals.) The recent discovery of the mammalian koala fish and the studies into its complex underwater chirping language and pouch manipulation has intensified the discussion. Scholars who used to think that whales, dolphins and sea-bats (the most common and well-known of the ocean mammals) were as smart as sea mammals could get, now agree that the koala fish is, without debate, at an entirely different and elevated intellectual level.

All that debate and discussion aside, nobody in history, ocean scientist or not, has ever mistaken the Pacific glan catfish for a rocket scientist. Not only do the two look nothing alike, but they are also as far apart as can be smartness-wise. So, when that certain curious, loner glan mutated due to excessive radiation, the thought of *MUST HAVE WHALE* was the first thought the glan catfish, or any fish of its species, had ever thought. That initial thought led to others and then others after that. At first the brainial influx was simple, to say the least. Basic messages such as, *WATER, COLD* and *LIGHT, ABOVE* and *WIGGLE AND SWIM*, evolved into a sort of warped, almost alien process of thinking and consciousness, far beyond what the celebrated koala fish could even imagine. Eventually, the glan was conducting what amounted to a running, internal dialogue.

I AM GLAN. I AM UNLIKE ANY OTHER FISH. OTHER FISH ARE NOT LIKE ME.
[SWIM, SWIM, SWIM.]
I AM IN THE MOOD FOR WHALE. I AM NOT CERTAIN AT THIS POINT IN TIME WHAT A WHALE IS, BUT I WILL KNOW IT WHEN I SEE IT. OH, LOOK AT THAT FISH. SLEEK. IF I AM NOT MISTAKEN, THE HUMANS (WHATEVER THEY ARE) CALL THIS FISH "BARRACUDA." THEY ARE HUNTERS. TO OTHER FISH THEY ARE DANGEROUS. NOT TO GLAN.
[SWIM, SWIM, SWIM.]

THAT SO-CALLED DANGEROUS FISH IS TOO CLOSE TO ME. I MUST MAKE HIM AN EXAMPLE FOR OTHERS LIKE HIM. LET'S SEE WHAT THESE DORSAL FIN IMPLEMENTS CAN DO. OH LOOK, A CORKSCREW. I WONDER WHAT THAT DOES. PERHAPS I CAN SPIN MY BODY AROUND AND THE CORKSCREW WILL SCARE AWAY THE ENEMY FISH.

[SPIN, SPIN, SPIN.]

WHOA, THAT WAS UNEXPECTED. THAT FISH HAS A HOLE IN IT AND IS FLOATING IN AN ASKEW MANNER. HE'S ALMOST AKIMBO. NO FISH IS THE FISH I AM.

[SWIM, SWIM, SWIM.]

LOOK AT THAT, A HAMMERHEAD SHARK. HA! ONE IMPLEMENT? I HAVE A DOZEN, PLUS MY BARBELS ARE MADE OF BALING WIRE. I BET THEY CAN DO SOME DAMAGE. I RECALL IT WAS A HAMMERHEAD SHARK THAT ATE MY BROTHER. I SHALL CALL MY EATEN BROTHER SAM. SURE, I HAD EIGHT HUNDRED AND FORTY-THREE BROTHERS, BUT SAM AND I WERE PARTICULARLY CLOSE. MY FAMILY WAS SCOFFED AT BY SO MANY OTHERS. WE WERE THE BOTTOM-FEEDERS, THE LOWLY CATFISH. NO MORE. ONCE I HAVE HAD MY FILL OF WHALE, I WILL NAIL THAT HAMMERHEAD. I WILL NAIL ALL HAMMERHEADS, AND THEN I WILL ELIMINATE THE SWORDFISH AND ALL OTHER FISH WITH TOOLS ATTACHED TO THEM. I AM GLAN AND I RULE THIS REALM.

[SWIM, SWIM, SWIM.]

I, GLAN, LOOK DOWN UPON ALL OTHERS IN THE OCEAN. KOALA FISH? WHAT KOALA FISH? I AM THE SMARTEST IN THE SEA. I AM THE MIGHTIEST. NONE ARE AS SMART OR AS MIGHTY AS ME, NOT EVEN THAT WHALE OVER THERE. WAIT, DID I SAY "WHALE" TO MYSELF? I DID! AT LONG LAST, A WHALE. AND NOW, THAT WHALE SHALL BE MINE.

And as the enlightened, maniacal and radiated fish dove deeper into his underwater adventure, he didn't notice (or perhaps did but didn't care) as the floating debris drifted overhead, now within a few hundred yards of the Pacific coastline, just south of the city the humans had named Bay City.

Officer Holstein had never before been up to the observation platform situated at the top of the spiral staircase that led up the interior of Canchim Tower. Once he took one look at the spectacular view, he made a mental note to head up to the site more often; at least more often than never.

From this vantage point, not only could the officer see out and across the bay to the north, and west to the ocean expanse, but also directly down to Lineback Street and the entire Mashona neighborhood. Basically, Officer Holstein could clearly see the entire route of his daily beat, but from an entirely different, non-sidewalk perspective. His gaze was immediately drawn to the rooftop of A China Shop, for obvious reasons. And, using that as a basis, a sort of focal point, the polite policeman filled in, in his mind, a mental overhead map of the neighborhood, identifying and labeling each location with a sort of mental pushpin.

Officer Holstein contemplated the view. *"Over there is the Toros Lawnmower Store, run by good 'ol Ankole Watusi. Once I own a lawn, I'll buy a lawnmower there, to be sure. And down there is that wonderful meat shop, the Offal House, where Mashona housewives and househusbands purchase the finest in tripe, gizzards and tongue, not to mention a multitude of curious edibles with which I am completely unfamiliar. Just down the street is the tiny Aceh Park with its spectacular fountain, packed with its regionally famous juggling goldfish. That round building adjacent to the park is the home of the Estonian Native Muumuu Shop. The owner claims they have the largest collection of tropical dresses anywhere in the lower forty-eight, and I bet she is probably correct, though I've never been inside the store."*

The mental pushpin for the next location, the Droughtmaster Plant Shop, was just about to be set in place in the mental map inside Officer Holstein's mind, when Ivory Chateaubriand spoke up, reminding the officer of why he was here in the first place.

"No, not that way, it's over here!" she said, with no shortage of urgency.

She reached atop her rather impressive hairdo to grab a pair of sunglasses, rapidly putting them on. Officer Holstein noticed she had five other pair still up there. He was a bit distracted by the sight and the implications thereof, a distraction that was whisked away by a sudden tug on his sleeve.

"Over here, Officer Holstein, look!" She pointed out to the southwest, off the shore and out in the ocean.

He couldn't see what she saw. There were a bunch of gulls circling around, but that was it.

"I'm so sorry, ma'am. I don't see anything," he admitted.

Ivory moved in closer and wrapped her arm around Holstein, hugging the officer. Several pair of her coif-topping sunglasses poked him in the right cheek. She slowly raised her left arm.

"There, follow my finger." She pointed. "Out in the water, just below those circling birds."

And there it was, so small in the distance that Officer Holstein couldn't figure out how she'd seen it in the first place, the thing that had inspired her so completely. It looked, from his perspective atop the sixty-foot tower, like a purple sea serpent was out in the ocean, surrounded by, or perhaps being escorted by, a flock of ocean birds.

"That looks like a purple sea serpent, Mrs. Chateaubriand!" Officer Holstein exclaimed.

"Are you crazy?" asked a suddenly agitated Ivory. "It doesn't look anything like a purple sea serpent. I think it's a gigantic floating eggplant headed directly this way. This is no joke. One of them ate up an entire city once, I read."

While Officer Holstein most certainly did not doubt his own sanity, he was beginning to doubt the sanity of one Ivory Chateaubriand, who had, seconds before removed, the sunglasses she was wearing, adding them back to her hair-top inventory.

"Where are my darn glasses?" she now fretted, her hands feeling all about her body, digging into her purse, scanning the platform and even tossing Officer Holstein a questioning and somewhat accusatory look.

Perhaps, he thought, it was those same sunglasses that made what was clearly a sea serpent look to Ivory like an eggplant. He attempted to calm the woman.

"I think that eggplant legend is probably just an old wise tale, ma'am," he began. "But, whatever it is, a sea serpent or an eggplant, it's purple and it is a threat. Thank you for pointing this out to me, Mrs. Chateaubriand, and have no fear. I will call this in and report it immediately."

And, as he headed back down the spiral staircase to street level, Officer Chris Holstein realized that he had no idea how in the heck he would go about doing that.

৸৸৸ ৸৸৸ ৸৸৸

While Officer Holstein was giving up trying to figure out how his two-way worked and opting to hoof it to his precinct down in Fishyman's Wharf, Devon Steerman had charts and graphs laid out across what seemed to be half of the carpeted floor of the basement of the Floral and Dance Sciences building at Aberdeen Angus University. Dr. Herens was there, rapt, but he was having a tough time following the young man's logic.

"Tell me again, Devon. How did you reach this conclusion?" the professor asked.

The student was claiming that the entirety of Bay City was about to be hit head-on by a deadly, devastating and clearly sudden cataclysmic storm.

"Well, when I run the biaxial line from the mean of the S&P run rate down through the current dew point and cross match it with Hinterwald, there is just no doubt. I don't know how exactly this is supposed to happen so suddenly, I just know that it is." Devon was focused, serious and determined. He truly believed what he was saying.

Dr. Herens couldn't argue with Devon's analysis, primarily because he couldn't understand any part of it. He thought about the budding weather and economy expert. The fledgling meteorolonomicist had blossomed into quite a convincing scientist. The professor thought back to the first time he'd met the bright student, fresh off the proverbial and literal dairy farm. The kindly professor was assigned to be Devon's guide and mentor, and to help him develop one of the crazy degree majors old Dean Malvi had dreamed up. Just thinking about how things had ended up – with apparent unrelated fields of study coming together to be not only of use to society but potentially lifesaving as well – made Herens chuckle. Who would have thought?

"This isn't funny, sir," Devon said, with a mix of consternation and concern. Clearly, he'd mistaken Herens' reflective musing for something it wasn't.

The professor decided it was time to act.

"Okay, Devon, this is what's going to happen," Herens began. "First, you are going to pick up all these papers. It's Bring Your Pet to Work Day today and I saw a wackadoodle puppy that I'm betting would love to do its business on any one of these sheets. Next, we're going to call the National Weather Association and let them in on your findings."

"All respect, sir," Devon countered. "They don't get any of this. It's all voodoo magic to them. They won't believe a word we tell them. It would be a big waste of time, and big time is something we just can't waste. Not now, anyway."

The professor wasn't exactly sure what Devon meant by that. He asked, "Well then, what do you suggest?"

"We need to call the media, and I mean now. This has to go out on the wire as soon as possible."

Dr. Herens mulled the idea over, dubious the media would take them seriously, particularly since, last he'd looked, glancing out his office window before heading downstairs, there wasn't a cloud in the sky. Still, Devon was so intensely determined. It wasn't likely he'd be persuaded to do anything other than reach out to the local media. Herens patted the young student on the shoulder.

"Okay, okay," he said softly. "We'll reach out to Channel Five News. I know one of the techs there. I mentored him in the mass media volleyball analysis major he was pursuing. But tell you what, let's not call this storm a hurricane."

"But it is a hurricane, Dr. Herens," Devon pleaded. "The charts don't lie."

"That's not what I mean, son," the professor assured him, surprised to find himself feeling convinced that Devon's conclusions, despite all visual evidence to the contrary, were correct. "What I mean is, most people don't use the word 'hurricane' when describing northern Pacific storms. They use the word 'typhoon.' So, we won't tell them that we're predicting a massive hurricane is going to appear out of nowhere and smash directly into Bay City. That would be preposterous. We're going to tell them a massive typhoon is going to do the same thing. Sound okay, Devon?"

"Sure does, sir," Devon replied, rapidly gathering up the multitude of storm evidence from the carpeted floor.

Though glad to have been able to teach him something new in this moment of crisis, Dr. Herens felt bad for the young scientist. Clearly Devon was scared. He imagined it must be tough to carry the torch and the weight and the burden of such financially and weatherly prescient knowledge.

His arms laden with all manner of research, Devon looked pleadingly at his valued guide. He asked, almost meekly, "While you are reaching out to Channel Five News, do you mind if I make a phone call? I've got to warn my dad."

"You do that, Devon," Dr. Herens kindly offered. "You do that."

〄〄〄

The Eastern Fincattle Nebula is one of recent discovery. An amateur astronomer in South Northwestern Central America discovered the cloudy cluster of stars while tracking the rare Evolene Comet some ten years back, and since then a furious debate has erupted among the astral-scientific community, including experts in cosmetology cosmology, about whether or not the worlds in the vicinity of the nebula are located in what is commonly referred to as the Golden Socks Zone. This region is believed to be ideal for supporting life, and intelligent life at that.

The swirling, dunce cap-shaped cloud that the Brain Trusters, Red Simford and, eventually, The Henchman saw in the eastern sky was no simple elevated and upside-down tornado. It was, in fact, an interstellar ship from one of those very same Fincattle Nebula neighborhood planetoids. Golden Socks Zone indeed.

Eventually the planetoid would come to be known as Planetoid Cowtune, but for now, as the craft twirled above the Centralized Valley, the Earth-bound humans below, both car salesmen and non-car salesmen, had no idea what to call the spinning object. Nor did they realize that extraterrestrials were responsible for what they still believed was an atmospheric anomaly.

Aboard ship were two crewmembers, both of whom bore an uncanny resemblance to common Hereford cows. Their species was dominant on their home planetoid, which had become dangerously overcrowded and polluted. The combination of too much population and too much methane gas had inspired the beings to seek out new life and new fertilization. A previous un-cowed mission had revealed Earth to be of extreme promise, with colonization possibilities abounding. Wasteful and unnecessary forests were being ripped up at breakneck speed and replaced with land perfect for grazing

"It's like they are preparing the planet for us to *moove* in," a presidential cow-being had pointed out, addressing the packed throng gathered udder to udder at the pre-dawn launch of the dunce cap-shaped spaceship. The throng mooed in agreement and happiness.

Later, above Earth, as the spacecraft hovered near the edge of the largest agricultural valley on the planet, scanning the region's soil makeup and air quality, its crewmembers discussed the bizarre coincidence that their planet-wide survey was revealing to them creatures already living here that looked virtually identical to themselves.

"What are the odds," mooed Crewmember One. "Of all the places and all the life in all the star systems, we come to a planet that has creatures that look just as we do?"

"It's a shame," mooed Crewmember Two, "that they are just so stupid. I mean, when I first saw that black and white guy with the huge horns I was all, 'Whoa! They don't make 'em like *that* back home.' But when we snuck down and I tried to speak to him, he simply stared off blankly, chewing gum." The lamentation was becoming a rant. "And what's up with that? Why does every single one of them spend all day chewing gum? And not only that, why is it that, when one of them turns and faces a different direction, they ALL turn and face the same direction?"

"Yep. Like you said," replied Crewmember One, "what a shame."

Crewmember One, who seemed to be the one in charge, took a look at the control panel readout, which had begun flashing symbols, numerals and colors on the screen in front of them. Once the readout was sufficiently mulled over, the current field analysis was pronounced concluded.

"Well, this report is complete and appears satisfactory," the first crewmember mooed. "This entire region looks perfect for expansion. Let's head to the next quadrant and see what we see."

And in an instant, the spacecraft darted up and to the east, like an Oriental hummingbird on amphetamines, out of sight of the spectators down at the Cow Palace.

Being the last of a dying breed, authentic cowboy John Steerman didn't much trust modern technology. He'd often yearn for the days of yore, when a man could rest easy with a bathroom located in an entirely different building than the living room, when dinner was poured from a can that had been opened with a brava knife and then dumped onto a tin plate, and when one man sold you both your shoe wax and your hair tonic in the same brown bottle. John didn't own a computer, and it was only because of the persistence of his son that he possessed one of those newfangled smartphones. The man would often joke that the devices were about as smart as a two-dollar pistol, though most folks had no clue to what he was referring.

But if Devon was anything he was convincing, as Professor Herens had just learned, and the young man had pestered his father to carry a phone on him at all times. In the end, John did indeed have a cell phone with him in case of emergencies. And an emergency was certainly brewing.

John waited the agreed upon twenty-two rings before answering the call. He despised salespeople, most relatives and such, and was bound and determined not to accidently pick up when one of them called. So the cowboy had made an arrangement with Devon that he would answer only after a dozen and ten rings. It rang that many times and so John, assured it was his son on the other end, answered.

"Yup," he said, his typical phone greeting.

"Dad, it's Devon. I've got to talk to you," the younger Steerman said.

His dad responded. "I figured that's why you called." He was in a rather chatty mood this day, quite unusual for him.

"Dad, there's a storm coming, a big storm, and it's heading directly toward Contented Corners. You, Caceres and Mrs. O'Leary have got to get out of there fast. Please, Dad, leave now."

John was taken aback, surprised by both his son's urgent tone and the critical information he'd just shared. He wasn't sure how to respond, so he answered with the comfortable, "Can't complain." That seemed to heighten both Devon's urgency and, luckily for all, his persistence.

"Dad, tell you what. Please put Mrs. O'Leary on the phone."

John became perplexed. He asked, "How in tarnation do I do that? She won't fit."

Exasperation was beginning to combine with urgency and persistence, and Devon replied, "Dad, go find Mrs. O'Leary, hand your phone over to her, and tell her I'd like to speak with her."

The youngster was not asking, John noticed.

John Steerman didn't like to be told to do anything, but his son was so darned insistent that the cowboy followed his directions to the word. After greeting Mrs. Margaret O'Leary with a tip of his imaginary hat and the customary "Ma'am," he handed the phone over to the kindly old lady. She figured this might be important, and opted to actually turn on her hearing aid, quite a rare activity for the woman. She found she could hear most of what the young man had to say.

Devon wasted no time in getting Mrs. O'Leary up to speed on his recent weather revelation. She loved the aspiring meteorology and finance expert, had helped raised him up, and always knew Devon to be a young man of the highest integrity.

She had to ask him to clarify a point or two about the imminent typhoon and then gave him a final, "Dang it, I knew it! My goiter is never wrong. I'll take care of it, Devon. You'd better get to safety yourself." She hung up and handed the phone back to John, looked him in the eyes and said sternly, "Now you listen to me, John Steerman." She hadn't used that phrase with him since he was in her first grade class, disrupting the other students with his infamous Donny Duck impersonation.

That got the cowboy's attention.

He thought briefly about bringing out the impersonation once again, just for old time's sake, but thought better of it and simply asked, "Ma'am?"

"John, there is a huge tycoon headed this way and we need to get out of Dodge."

John missed the allusion, quite surprising with him being a real cowboy and all. Margaret could see the confusion wash over him. Hoping to avoid yet another questioning "Ma'am," she continued, as urgently now as Devon had just been on the phone.

"We've got to leave, and leave in a hurry. Your son didn't say where to go other than inland, so let's just head for the Centralized Valley. Do you get me, John? We've got to get out of here."

The elder Steerman tipped his imaginary hat. Mrs. O'Leary took that to mean he understood.

She continued, taking charge of the evacuation proceedings. "You find Caceres and round up the cattle and load them onto the flatbed. I'll grab a chicken or two and get the aardvarks and get them into the back of the pickup. I think I can still drive that thing." Mrs. O'Leary hadn't been behind the wheel of a vehicle in over a decade.

John was still looking a bit confused, but had managed to put his smartphone back into his shirt pocket.

"Go on, John. You've got to move now."

One last tip of the invisible hat and a final "Ma'am," and John turned and headed back to the barn.

Margaret O'Leary glanced over toward the pond, the usual hangout for the aardvarks, thinking to herself, *"I'm sure Devon is correct, but what the heck does the weather have to do with some big rich guy?"*

ᗩᑎᗩ ᗩᑎᗩ ᗩᑎᗩ

As Mrs. O'Leary carefully searched the pond area of Contented Corners, looking for aardvarks, Staff Sergeant Anjoni Jones shuffled through her duty roster, trying to determine exactly who the extremely polite and a tad agitated police officer at her desk was. He'd burst through the front door of Precinct Seventeen minutes before, apologizing to everyone he made eye contact with for the suddenness of his interruption, before eventually being directed to this location to, as he insisted rather vehemently he must do, file a report.

"Tell me your name again, Officer," Sgt. Jones said.

"It's Holstein, kind woman. Police Officer Deputy Chris Holstein. And, if you please, I've got to file a report. The whole city could be in grave danger."

"Holstein, Holstein..." The staff sergeant scanned her squad-of-the-day report. "Nope, no Holstein here. We've got a Holster. Are you Officer Holster?" She asked.

"This delay is costing valuable time," Officer Holstein thought. He explained, "I've got the beat up the hill near Canchim Tower. In the Mashona neighborhood, if you please."

Sgt. Jones thought this man might be the most polite person she'd ever met. She felt sorry for him, for some reason. Kindly she continued, "Look, deary, your name and that beat aren't anywhere in my paperwork. But why did you run all the way down here? You could have just called in this... this threat or whatever it is."

Holstein was embarrassed to admit he hadn't quite got the handle of how to use his two-way. He lied, "This was just too important to put over the airwaves, m'lady. I needed to get this information down here in person."

He didn't mention the fact that he had to ask several folks how to find the building. He couldn't remember ever having set foot in the place.

"Well, I can take your report, if you like," Sgt. Jones suggested.

"Umm, well I don't mean to offend. That's the one thing I hate to do more than anything," Chris replied. "But is there a Lieutenant or General or someone I could speak with? This is most assuredly quite important."

The staff sergeant was beginning to think that perhaps this gentleman, though he was a gentleman, might not be the sharpest knife in the deck. "Hon, this is the Bay City Police Department, not the army. Besides, I'm in charge around here right now. Everyone else is out to lunch. Why don't you just tell me what in the world is going on."

"Well, okay then," Officer Holstein answered.

And then, speaking in a quiet tone so as to not cause precinct-wide hysteria, he told the staff sergeant about getting an automated call on his two-way and meeting Ivory Chateaubriand at the base of Canchim Tower. He recounted climbing the spiral staircase and the spectacular view of the quaint shops along Lineback Street. And then, after cautioning Sgt. Jones that the information he was about to share was shocking and quite terrifying, he explained in great detail, checking his small spiral notepad frequently to ensure accuracy, the circling seabirds and the floating object that was most likely a purple sea serpent (though it being an eggplant was not out of the question). After he outlined the entire tale in an effective and accurate manner, he took a step back and snapped to attention, just as he'd been taught to do years ago back at the academy.

Staff Sergeant Anjoni Jones stared at the rigid policeman in disbelief. She wasn't sure what to make of the kind, funny beat cop. He was certainly earnest, and it was clear he believed what he was telling her, as ridiculous as it sounded. And then it struck her – the good officer was awaiting instructions.

The staff sergeant took a few moments to regather her composure, cleared her throat, and said, "Thank you, Officer Holstein. You have done a great job so far, but I think the best thing for you to do now is to head back to your position, and with urgency. Calm the good people in that neighborhood. They need your steady hand, they need your authority and direction."

"Yes, sir!" Officer Holstein saluted, and then bowed in a large and theatrical way, as was his habit.

This caught the staff sergeant as off guard as had his story about the purple menace. She needed the man out of her precinct as soon as possible.

Again regrouping, she replied, "I can have one of our patrolmen give you a lift back up the hill. They've got squad cars and everything."

"Oh, no. Thank you, but I don't believe in them, Staff Sergeant." Officer Holstein was already heading for the exit doors. The man certainly knew how to follow directions. Sgt. Jones called out to him, "We'll handle a coordinated response from here, Officer Holstein. Good luck to you, and thank you again."

Officer Chris Holstein either didn't want to know or didn't care about how the Bay City Police Department was going to officially respond to what in his mind would best be called "The Eggserpent." All he knew was that the people of Mashona Town needed him now more than ever and he wasn't about to disappoint a single one of them.

And as Staff Sergeant Jones considered the previous few minutes of her life, she thought to herself, *I need a drink.*

꠸꠸ ꠸꠸ ꠸꠸

Dutch Friesian believed in the old adage, "It's better to beg for permission than forgive when asking." He wasn't sure exactly how the saying went, but he believed in it. The phrase had long served him well, whether he was cleaning up after elephants, making a wonderful cup of Earl Pekoe Chameleon tea, or, as was the case in this case, arranging the entertainment as part of an evil plot to take down the national leader in Tauros auto sales.

So, as the small group standing outside of the Cow Palace continued to look up into the midday sky, The Henchman, rightly, swelled with pride as he watched the entertainers he had booked for the event step out of a shared taxi. The three of them looked spectacular. Fulani Fruitcakes mascot Herbie the Heifer, known to his mother as Brad, stood in full brown cow costume, minus the cow head, which he carried under his left arm. Bullfighter extraordinaire Salers Salorn, just back from his book-signing tour of the Centralized Valley, wore the traditional garb of his homeland, the jewel-encrusted miniature bassoons hanging from his tunic sparkling in the bright sunlight. And there was Siri Batangas, sporting an outrageous powdered wig and swimming trunks, both clearly being worn inside out.

The trio of performers had come up from behind the tiny group of sky-gazers and had joined them in scanning the eastern horizon. Nobody other than The Henchman had noticed them there when Siri spoke up, in a voice reminiscent of a famous old-time movie star.

"I say, what in the world are we looking at?"

His comment startled Red and the Brain Trusters.

"What the...!" Simford blurted out. He turned around excitedly and was stunned when it turned out the voice came from an unexpected source. An oversized smile crossed his face. "Well, don't that beat all!" Red said excitedly. "You got me there, you did!" He grabbed the impressionist's hand and shook vigorously. "You must be that Baltanger feller The Henchman, er, I mean Dutch told me about!"

The celebrity impersonator nodded a greeting. "Siri Batangas at your service. And you must be that red person Mr. Friesian referred to. The pleasure is mine."

Red continued, shaking his head in astonishment. "That is amazing. When you talk normal it's like you don't have any accent. But when you talked before and I wasn't looking, it was like that actor guy, that Symons Type feller, was right here, even though he's been dead for thirty years."

The Henchman thought that Batangas was impersonating the movie icon Gir Gobra, but he kept that opinion to himself. He could tell the star was happy he'd impressed the man with the checkbook.

Batangas repeated his original question. "I say, what in the world were you folks looking at?"

Red laughed at the uncanny mimicry before him, and then waved off the question. "Oh, it was nothing. Some sort of weird cloud, but it's gone now." Then he looked at the other two gentlemen. "Okay, now don't tell me, which of you is the cow mascot?"

ᓚᘏᗢ ᓚᘏᗢ ᓚᘏᗢ

History would record that Typhoon Bessie was the first-ever storm to hit a populated city on the Pacific side of the Northern Hemisphere. Scientists of all types considered such weather occurrences impossible, and this storm, with its high winds and dramatic ocean surge, further surprised weather experts by appearing apparently out of nowhere.

Long-time Bay City meteorologist, Channel Five News' Bo Vine, later reported that someone from a local university had offered up shouts of warning minutes before the storm formed a few miles offshore, but that the dire predictions were not taken seriously. With the high winds, heavy rain and extensive flooding knocking out power for much of the city so soon after the storm made landfall, there wasn't much anyone could have done to prevent the widespread destruction caused by the freak storm. Typhoon Bessie did indeed hit Bay City head-on.

Bizarre cloud formations, reported by some in the region, have been named as the trigger for the storm's sudden appearance. Another source given was the unusual El Niña Niño La Noonya offshore flow in the ocean, where the water was over eighty degrees in some places, and below forty degrees just a few dozen feet away. The expansion of global ozone warming layers has also been theorized as a possible cause, but in the end, the fact of the matter is, nobody really knows what caused Typhoon Bessie.

And once the storm subsided and power was restored, nightly news programs throughout the country reported on the enormity of the devastation: the washed-out buildings, collapsed towers, flooded neighborhoods and dramatic rescues that occurred during the height of the typhoon. However, those reports didn't paint the entirety of the picture. They didn't describe the horrors of mutation that were observed during the cataclysm. Not that anyone would have believed what happened in the midst of the nightmare.

What had begun as a typical, happy day under clear skies, changed with a sickening suddenness into a day of tragedy, misery and chaos.

Utter chaos.

PART TWO:

THE MUTATION

I N THE TIME IT TOOK Mrs. O'Leary to round up all the aardvarks she could find and lead them into the back of the old Tauros pickup, the sky had clouded over and it had begun to rain quite heavily. She couldn't recall the weather ever having turned so nasty so fast. Drenched by the sudden downpour, she darted into her shack and put on some galoshes and a slicker. Not wanting to waste any time, she dashed back out to begin a quick search for a chicken or two. She wasn't too concerned about the fowl, and had an idea that they were some of the smartest creatures at Contented Corners. She figured they could fend for themselves, regardless of how bad this big tycoon was, whenever it was he showed up. The little birds would most likely fly away or hide out in the storm cellar if they got too riled up. She was certain there was a storm cellar around the farm somewhere. With all of this in mind, Mrs. O'Leary took a quick look down the false-bottom well and behind the mailbox, but couldn't find Chicken One. She'd taken to numbering the cute little egg-layers once there were more than four of them in the flock, and Chicken One was her favorite. She was about to call out "Here, Chicken One!" but suddenly thought better of it and decided to check on John.

Now that she thought about it (and not about aardvarks and chickens), she hadn't seen or heard from John since she sent him back to round up the cows, so absorbed was she in her own emergency preparations. With the rain's intensity on the increase and a wind beginning to whip up, Margaret headed back to the farmhouse. She approached from the side, and when she walked around the front of the building, she was stunned to see John Steerman, sitting on the wooden rocking chair on the porch, whittling. It looked like he was carving a yeti. He glanced up, noticed Mrs. O'Leary in her rubber raingear and shocked expression, and moved to tip his imaginary hat.

She stopped him mid-tip, quite upset with the current state of affairs. "John Steerman, don't you tip and 'ma'am' me. What in the world are you doing?"

"I'm carvin' a yeti, ma'am," the man responded. He seemed quite proud of his creation.

The now-soaked woman responded sternly, "John, I told you to get the cows and put them in the back of the flatbed. What part of 'there is a giant tycoon headed this way' did you not understand?"

John answered simply, "All of it."

That appeared obvious to the nearly frantic woman. "John, where the heck is Caceres? I told you to have him help you."

John nodded toward the flatbed, adding the familiar, "Ma'am." The man, it seemed, just could not help himself.

At first, Margaret hadn't noticed the diminutive Andalusian immigrant, but there he was, loading something onto the flatbed. It most certainly was not a cow. The water was starting to puddle up in various places around the farm, so Mrs. O'Leary had to practically slog her way the twenty yards over to the transport vehicle, which was parked just outside the open barn door. When she got to the truck, Margaret was surprised once again. While he wasn't whittling or anything close to it, the tiny man was putting armfuls of flowering plants, apparently tugged right out of the ground, onto the flat surface of the flat bed.

"What the heck are you doing, Caceres?" Mrs. O'Leary asked.

"I load my plants so the gigantic python not get them, miss."

"You are doing what so what?" the woman queried, incredulous.

"Mr. Steer say that gigantic python come and we must get cows and leave. I save my flowers too. See, I push them forward so cows fit." Caceres reached into the flatbed and slid the assorted colorful vegetation up against the back of the cab.

Before Mrs. O'Leary could respond, two bolts of lightning cracked down at the exact same time, on either side of the dirt driveway, down by the gate. After the bright flash and explosive thunder, the sky in that direction, across Highway One and out above the Pacific, seemed to turn a dark and ominous shade of purple. Margaret shivered and cinched her slicker tight. The wind began to increase in intensity, the rain now coming down in proverbial sheets and at quite an acute angle.

"No more flowers, Caceres," Margaret directed. "You get the loading ramp hooked up to the back of this thing, and I'll head into the barn and bring the cows out. Then you get them up there and tie 'em in good. Do you understand, Caceres?"

"Sí," was all the small immigrant said, and in a flash he dashed back to the toolshed to grab the truck ramp.

Throughout it all, John Steerman whittled away, nearly finished with his miniature yeti.

ᓫᒡᐳᓫᒡᐳᓫᒡᐳ

"Wow, that came on in a hurry," thought Officer Holstein as he finally made it to the top of the switchbacks and stood looking at the Lineback Business District.

When the policeman had begun the trek up the famous serpentine roadway, it had been a bright and sunny day. Now that the officer had made it up to the top, the sky was completely clouded over and it was raining heavily. It was as if the storm had come out of nowhere.

But this was no time for the good officer to think about the weather, as he had been tasked with protecting the people of the Mashona neighborhood. He looked down the four-block stretch of businesses that led south and ended at Canchim tower, barely visible in the newborn storm. Officer Holstein figured that issuing complete and total evacuation orders to all of the businesses on the boulevard would be the best way to proceed, particularly since a good many of the area's rich yuppies would be, at present, shopping in those very same businesses.

With time both critically short and of the essence, Holstein decided to get a cup of coffee. As luck would have it, the first establishment at the top of the switchbacks was the combination diner and petting zoo, the Calfeteria. He headed toward the door just as Ivory Chateaubriand was headed out, and the two nearly bumped into one another, coming dangerously close to spilling Ivory's skinny tall no-sugar medium-low-fat espressachino latte. The polite officer spent the next several minutes bowing and apologizing profusely to Ivory. She had practically finished the drink when he stopped mid-bow, an idea suddenly flashing in his mind like one of those old-timey flashbulbs.

"Mrs. Chateaubriand, perhaps it is no accident that has brought us together a second time today. I think I could really use your help."

Ivory Chateaubriand had long considered herself an amateur detective. She could solve those jumble puzzles they used to have in the local newspaper almost every time. Plus, she loved watching reruns of the once-popular television mystery, *Murder, She Dictated.*

"Why, I'd be delighted to help," she answered with a wide smile. "Anything, just name it."

Officer Holstein nodded. He explained about his trip to the local precinct and his assignment to calm the people of the neighborhood.

Ivory interrupted. "But everyone seems calm to me." And added, using her above-average deductive skills, "Except for the few I see scurrying to get out of the rain."

The policeman hadn't noticed any scurrying taking place, and thought that perhaps that the multi-sunglass-adorned woman was perfect for what he had in mind. This lady was sharp.

The officer continued, "Well, they aren't uncalm right now, but imagine their terror if they knew that a giant purple sea serpent, or perhaps even an eggplant, was headed directly this way. They wouldn't be so calm then, I can assure you."

"I never thought of it like that," she replied. "I guess that's why you are the policeman and I am the housewife."

They both chuckled a little at this, but then the officer replied somberly, "I've been through the training, Mrs. Chateaubriand, I've seen things."

Ivory nodded in understanding, trying to keep the thought of the things this officer had seen as far from her mind as possible.

She changed the subject. "So, what can I do to help?"

Officer Holstein sighed, as if that would aid in his determination. He explained, "Well, I have got to evacuate the entire region. All of these businesses need to shut down, to board up if they're capable, and all the yuppies, er, I mean shoppers, need to get home and hunker down."

The officer and Ivory continued their conversation in what had turned into a driving rainstorm. A garbage can blew across the roadway and began to roll down the switchbacks.

Holstein continued, "The thing is, Mrs. Chateaubriand, I'm only one police officer and I am afraid I just won't have the time to get everyone out before it's too late."

"Too late for what?" the woman asked.

"Too late before the unimaginable happens. Be that sea serpent, which I suspect, or the much less likely but still possible eggplant."

College-educated Ivory Chateaubriand found herself shocked that the Bay City Police Department would send only one overly polite police officer deputy to handle a situation of this magnitude. But then again, perhaps this was just an average, ordinary giant-sized city-eating floating eggplant. The man, after all was the law, and she had been raised to respect people in positions of authority.

After a moment of consideration, she offered, "I'd be happy to help warn folks."

"That's exactly what I was thinking," Holstein responded, pondering to himself, *"Is this woman a mind reader too?"*

A unicycle tumbled past the two, dangerously close, headed down the street toward Canchim tower, followed by an unmanned pogo stick, haphazardly hopping as if following the unicycle. This was most assuredly one bizarre storm, and any doubts that Officer Holstein may have had about the need for a complete evacuation were totally dashed. He considered this almost-collision a near miss, and promptly recommended the two of them duck inside the Calfeteria to continue their conversation.

There, he went on. "Mrs. Chateaubriand, it's been a while since I've done this, but I think I recall the process from back at the academy."

"Do what?" Ivory asked, a bit puzzled.

"My lady, I need to deputize you."

The housewife was a bit stunned, and asked, "You're going to do what?"

Holstein answered. "I am going to deputize you. That way people will believe you when you tell them they need to evacuate." The officer scanned the Calfeteria, looking for something. With no instant luck, he asked, "You don't happen to have a Bible on you, do you?"

She began to reply, "I'm sure we don't need a..." but in an instant Officer Holstein was up on a chair, his right arm extended out, official badge in hand.

"Good people," he said loudly. "My name is Officer Deputy Chris Holstein and I need to ask, do any of you kind folks happen to have in your possession a bible of any kind?"

There were only a handful of people, some moms and kids, in the combination diner and petting zoo, and they all knew and loved the kindly beat cop. He needn't have wasted his time with an introduction, impressive though it was.

A smartly dressed woman seated at a table covered with brightly colored and informative magazines, reached into her bag and pulled out a Bible. "I've got one here, Officer Holstein," she said.

He hopped off the chair and walked toward the woman, giving her one of his patented theatrical bows. "Thank you, my good woman!" he said.

Bible in hand, he returned to Ivory Chateaubriand who, as luck would have it, had finally finished her drink. She needed both hands for the swearing-in that was about to occur, and having a paper cup in one hand might have slowed down the proceedings a bit, something that could have had tragic consequences considering what was at stake. Officer Holstein instructed her to put one hand on the Bible and one hand on her heart. It took some finagling before he realized he actually had to hold the book so that the soon-to-be assistant deputy could put her hand on it.

Officer Holstein began the swearing in. "Ivory Chateaubriand, do you solemnly swear to uphold the laws of the city of Bay City to the best of your abilities, so help you?"

"I do." Ivory Chateaubriand hadn't said those words since her wedding day.

"I now pronounce you Assistant Deputy Ivory Chateaubriand."

A youngster playing with a duck in the corner of the diner stopped his activity, stood upright and began to clap. Soon everyone in the place was joined in a round of applause. Officer Holstein picked this opportunity to let the folks know what was up. He stepped back up on the chair.

"Ladies and gentlemen, boys and girls. We need to evacuate the premises. There is a significant threat headed to this vicinity and you would all do me a tremendous favor in leaving now."

The clapping sort of died down, and the patrons and servers stared at each other in disbelief, wondering what to do next.

New Assistant Deputy Ivory Chateaubriand also got up on a chair. Since Holstein hadn't climbed down from his, they both were towering above the folks in the Calfeteria.

She clarified things. "Listen and listen good. There is some freaky gigantic eggplant headed straight toward us, and if you don't want yourself or your children to be squished or eaten, I recommend you leave now."

The people continued to look bewildered, but at least a few were milling around. The smartly dressed woman retrieved her Bible from the table next to the assistant deputy. Clearly people were not evacuating at anything near the rate Ivory had hoped. Before he knew what was what, Ivory reached over and grabbed Officer Holstein's weapon. She raised her hand and fired the stun gun right into the ceiling. The wired projectile ricocheted around a bit in the overhead fluorescents before shorting out some vital connection, shutting the lights off in the entire building.

From the darkness, the assistant deputy shouted, "I SAID OUT, FOOLS. GET OUT NOW!"

That did the trick, and soon Assistant Deputy Ivory Chateaubriand and Officer Chris Holstein were alone, in the dark, standing on chairs. They could hear the wind and rain pounding on the outside of the building. Holstein had the idea that the deputizing may have gone to Ivory's head, just a bit. The officer glanced at his new associate, who stood holding the stun gun and tracing the fired tip up the now-harmless wire and into the dark overhead fixtures.

"Mrs. Chateaubriand, may I have my gun back?" he asked. The stun gun was the only weapon Holstein carried, if you didn't count his nightstick and his industrial-sized can of mace.

"Why, sure," the woman answered, with a kind and wide smile. "And you don't have to call me 'Mrs. Chateaubriand' anymore."

"I don't?" Holstein asked, now a bit wary of the decision he'd made to recruit the lady.

"No, not at all. Assistant Deputy Chateaubriand will do just fine."

Though polite, the folks at Channel Five News were no help at all. They weren't about to go live and interrupt their showing of the classic movie *Hidee* with a newsflash regarding a sudden superstorm, be that storm a typhoon or hurricane.

Back down in the basement of the Floral and Dance Sciences building, Devon Steerman pleaded with Dr. Herens to give their plan to warn people another try.

"Can't we just call another station?" he asked. "Someone is bound to believe us eventually."

"Son," Dr. Herens responded, "We could call the media until the cows come home. Nobody is going to believe that the city is in such imminent danger. And when you think about it, what good would it do? If this thing pops up as quickly as your research says it will, people won't have time to do much about it anyway." The teacher stared off, a great sense of helplessness washing over him.

"We've got to try, Dr. Herens." Devon just wouldn't take no for an answer and hopped to his feet. Inspiration had hit him. "Professor, any idea where we can find a bullhorn?"

Though Dr. Herens had no idea what Devon was up to, he did, in fact, have a bullhorn up in his office. He'd bought one when it appeared he'd be mentoring a student in another combination major, this one joining rowing and commercial cupcake baking. He'd figured that, at the very least, the device could be used when he occupied the coxswain position in a boat and needed to shout out encouragement. And, he'd reasoned, you never know when a bullhorn might come in handy in an industrial bakery.

He answered the young man, "Well, Devon, as luck would have it, I happen to have a bullhorn upstairs in my office. What do you have in mind?"

But, before Devon could answer, there was a large "CLANK" and all the lights in the basement suddenly went out. Devon could tell right away this was not just a lighting problem caused by some random stun gun being fired into the overhead fluorescent fixtures. The little power light on his desktop computer array was dark as well.

"Dr. Herens," he said confidently, "it's a power outage."

The teacher couldn't remember if the Floral and Dance Sciences building had a backup generator, but he doubted it. Devon, a firm believer that it was best to be prepared to ensure small emergencies don't become big disasters, flicked on his combination flashlight, radio, alarm, phone charger and electric razor. He kept it next to his computer system, always within reach.

He was extremely proud of his preparedness efforts, and rightly so, bragging a bit to the professor, "I could shave right now if I wanted to, Dr. Herens."

Though impressed, Herens thought they had more important issues to deal with than Devon's five o'clock shadow, which, if the young man had one, was completely unnoticeable.

The professor addressed his immediate concern. "Devon, you don't think that the storm has already hit, do you? That might explain the power outage."

"It's surely possible, if not probable, Dr. Herens," Devon responded. "We should head upstairs and see what's up."

"Good idea," the professor replied. "You've got the light, you lead the way." The room was pitch black except for the circle of brightness provided by the flashlight. Devon headed off in the direction of the elevator, and, realizing the power to that was probably out too, took a left near the foosball table and headed for the stairs.

When they were about ten feet away from venturing up and out of the basement, a three-foot wall of water came careening around a bend in the stairs, directly at them. They scampered back to the foosball table to assess the situation.

Water began pouring into the basement through the stairway up to street level, their only way out. It already had knocked over a couple of cubicles, which the pair could see in the light from Devon's flashlight. Then a series of loud crashes, three in succession, rocked the building, startling both the student and his mentor. Next came two successive thunder claps, one after another, and then a humongous smashing sound as if something quite large had collapsed. It seemed like the very building the two were in was under attack.

"Well, Professor," Devon said, "I guess the typhoon has started. And not only that, we're trapped."

🐂 🐂 🐂

Red Simford figured there was no point in delaying this spectacular, or any regular old car-selling extravaganza. So, once the introductions were made and he was able to accurately discern which entertainer was which, Red officially announced the Cow Palace Tauros Spectacular Car Show open for business.

In addition to the cars fanned out in front of the arena like the rays of the sun, the lot was lousy with balloons, streamers, colorful signage and all other sorts of car-selling paraphernalia typical to these types of events. Red carpets led down every row, sloping toward the square concrete building that sat in the center of the bowl where the salesmen – and they were all men – could lead prospective customers to the finance department, set up on several picnic tables inside the arena proper.

Red assigned the performers their respective tasks. Salers Salorn, the famous bullfighter, was stationed near the Tauros truck section. He brought out his bright cape and swished it around as he traveled in between the trucks. Brad, the cow mascot, was dispatched to the nearby main thoroughfare, Guzerat Street, where he was to wave and moo at passing traffic, directing folks into the parking lot. Meanwhile, the celebrity impersonator, Siri Batangas, dove right into his routine, deftly executed on an impressive stage that had been erected just for him in the middle of the crossover convertible three-wheel drive sedan section. The talented performer brought out his A-game from the get-go. Dressed in a fancy tux, he launched into a hilarious skit where he played all three members of the internationally famous Barzona Trio. He nailed the impersonations and, had anyone been there to witness the performance, they most certainly would have enjoyed it.

Red considered himself to be the most important cog in the entertainment wheel. He donned his twenty-gallon hat, waxed up his oversized handlebar mustache and climbed behind the wheel of his custom-made Tauros. The beast of a car was one-of-a-kind, made especially for Red Simford, partially in thanks for the incredible job he'd done over the years selling Tauroses. While the vehicle, named the Cattle-ac for a good number of reasons, couldn't travel any faster than molasses on an ice floe, it didn't need to. Red loved to make the rounds of his car lot back home, and would steer the huge convertible carefully so as not to puncture car buyers or salesmen with the grill-mounted horns. He'd wave and greet the shoppers, who appreciated his oversized demeanor and impressive vehicle.

Now the man backed his conveyance down the loading ramp of the transport semi, and began his circumnavigation of the Cow Palace parking area, just as it began to rain.

"That's funny," the mustached man thought. "We had clear skies just a little bit ago."

And this was no light shower; the rain came on strong under the darkest of skies, and so Red decided it would be best to park the convertible under the large, permanent awning that protruded out over the arena ticket windows. He figured he'd just wait until this storm blew over. Red took the opportunity to call The Henchman over for a brief chat. He'd caught sight of his number two man involved in what appeared to be a heated discussion with one of the Brain Trusters. Once Red got out of the rain and out of the Cattle-ac, he called and motioned for The Henchman to join him at the car's rear bumper. The former Weasel headed over, looking quite agitated.

"What's the problem, The Henchman?" Red asked.

"That idiot Pinzgauer or Podalica or whatever his name is, you know, that guy from Jersey? He's an idiot," Dutch belted out.

"Okay, we've established he's an idiot," Red replied. "So, what's the problem?"

Dutch Friesian explained, "This guy, this idiot guy, he says he got a call from one of his friends who lives near here who told him we need to close down the car sale."

"Close down the car sale?" Red asked. "Well that's a bunch of bullpucky. Why in the world would we do that? We're just getting started. In fact, I was just thinking we really need to beef up the entertainment if we're going to counteract all of this rain."

The Henchman replied, "This guy's friend says his brother is in this biker gang and they are headed this way. It can't be good, Pulikulam or Ponwar or whatever his name is said. He said he's getting out of here."

It was then that a distant but fast-approaching roar was heard. Within a few seconds, a long line of motorbikes, some forty or fifty long, came rolling and roaring through the rain down Guzerat Street, turning directly into the Cow Palace parking lot. It took a couple moments more before the entire train of bikes had rolled on in, most of them riding right up under the awning and next to the serious-looking Red and the astonished The Henchman. As the bikers dismounted, Red could see they wore the leathers of an authentic gang. The backs of their jackets were adorned with the image of a skull, a sword and a microwave oven. Underneath the terrifying, spectacular and somewhat confusing image was one word, in blood-red bold letters: "Horro."

A tall and muscular man of about sixty who appeared to be the leader of the gang walked slowly up to Red and Dutch. He had a three-inch scar in the direct center of his forehead and a weathered face that looked a lot like tanned hide. Clearly this man had been through a lot.

He spoke without making eye contact with either of the two men, staring off in the general direction of the performance stage. "I am Pajuna. We are the Horro. We are here for the tattoos."

Red was obviously baffled by the man's statement. He replied, "We don't have any tattoos, we have cars. A lot of cars. The best selection of the incredible Tauros automobile anywhere in the region."

He stepped toward the biker, motioning as if he was going to put a hand on the man's shoulder, an international sign that means "I'm going to try to sell you something now."

Pajuna took a corresponding step backwards. Red took another step forward, right arm extended. Pajuna took another step back.

This continued for a couple more steps until the gang leader, reaching for a sheath at his hip, shouted, "Wait!"

Everyone froze.

Pajuna asked, "What do you mean you don't have tattoos? We came for the tattoos. We want the tattoos."

The Henchman suddenly figured out what was going on and stopped the eye-darting he'd been doing for the last several moments as Red and Pajuna faced one another. "Boss, I know what's going on. I just remembered."

He then started toward the biker, and several other bikers, clearly awaiting their own tattoos, growled aloud. A few of them reached for assorted sheaths and holsters. One of them pressed the horn button on his chopper. It beeped.

Dutch knew he'd literally gone far enough. He stopped in his tracks and tried to explain, nervously, to all involved in what had turned into a standoff. "Mr. Pajuna, sir," he began. "The tattoo, lawn, garden, and ballpoint pen convention that was supposed to start today has been rescheduled. Our company reserved this place to sell cars. That's what we are doing. There are no tattoos here today, sir, but I'd be happy to make you all a nice cup of tea."

Red had to admit, he'd made the right choice in naming this guy The Henchman. He was downright wily.

The leader of the Horro thought about what Dutch had just said and gave a nod back to the bikers gathered about, most of whom now wore relieved expressions.

He spoke again. "The Horro like cars. We stay."

At that, the entire gang dismounted and began to move toward the lines of automobiles. Several Brain Trusters appeared in a flash to assist in the car buying experience.

As soon as he could tell all was well, Red turned and faced The Henchman. What should have been a happy countenance was not at all a happy countenance. Red was incensed.

"The Henchman," he growled. "Where in the heck is that cow... boy?" Red purposefully paused between the words so as not to give the impression he considered Brad the mascot to be a genuine cowboy. He continued. "When those guys came riding in here he was not up on the roadway where he's supposed to be."

"Well, I don't know, boss." Dutch replied. "But I will sure find out!"

Red was nearly ballistic. "Great, and when you do, then track down that Baltanger feller. He's not on his stage. Here we have a whole herd of live ones, drove right in and ripe for the pickin', and these dang entertainers you got aren't entertaining. You best get with it, or I'll get with it with you. You got me?"

While Dutch had no clue what Red meant by it, he considered that last part of the man's rant both a threat and a promise. "I'm on it, boss."

And though he didn't know where to begin his search for the wayward performers, he knew that the origin point for his exploration had to be out of eyesight of Red Simford. Friesian dashed around a corner of the arena and headed to the section of the lot dedicated to selling Tauros trucks.

Salers Salorn was in the middle of the trucks, standing in the bed of one of the pickups. The infamous bullfighter was grandly swishing his colorful cape, much to the delight of a pair of bikers who'd positioned themselves on the hoods of a couple of nearby rigs. The duo clapped and *oohed* in delight as Salorn seemingly defied gravity with his spectacular cape swishing. Dutch scooted up to the performer, interrupting briefly to ask the man if he'd seen the two missing entertainers. The Spanish European gave a grand swish in the direction of a long RV parked at the back of the lot, behind the vehicles. Amidst more appreciative applause from the tiny audience, The Henchman darted off toward the RV.

During sales events, and on some holidays, the Brain Trusters used the fully loaded Tauros Danish Black-Pied RV (abbreviated DBP) as a combination breakroom, game room and den. The Henchman loved to make tea for folks in the DBP. While most RVs feature a tiny mini-kitchen of some sort, the DBP had all the bells and whistles any tea brewer or cook, particularly one partial to barbecuing, could ask for. Teamaking, typically in the forefront of The Henchman's thoughts, was far from his mind at this particular moment. The Henchman stood in the RV's doorway in disbelief. Both mascot and celebrity impersonator were staring at the wide-screen television mounted on the front wall.

Before Dutch could speak, Siri Batangas called out to him, in that uncanny accent he'd used when first introducing himself to Friesian and the others. "I say, be a good man and shut that door. It's getting frighteningly stormy out."

The mimic was right; the wind had begun to howl.

Dutch stepped inside, slamming the door behind him. "What are you guys doing in here? Red is spitting mad at you. You've got to get back to work!"

"We are watching this delightful movie, my good man," Siri answered cheerfully, still in character.

Brad, dressed in full outfit, with his cow head in place, added, "Yeah, man. We're on lunch. Or, wait," he said, getting into the old-time movie spirit of things. "I mean, we're having tea. It's teatime."

Now, The Henchman was torn. He knew he should chastise the men for basically abandoning their posts in the sales yard. But, by golly, these two not only had no tea, they most likely had no clue how to make a quality pot. They most assuredly had no idea where in the DBP the tea was kept, not to mention the kettle and cozy.

Several minutes later, the three men were enjoying cups of piping hot and refreshing Honeybush Chai Oolong tea, one of Dutch's favorite blends. They were all closely following the adventures of the little girl in the black and white movie, *Hidee*. Every time the little girl spoke, Siri Batangas would repeat her line, trying his best to get her tone and accent just right.

The curly-haired girl would ask, "But grandfather, do I really have to ride a donkey to Danish Europe?" Then The Henchman and Brad would look at Siri, who would parrot the exact same line back to the TV.

"Oh, you've almost got it now, Siri," the cow mascot exclaimed excitedly.

"I'll say you do," offered up Dutch, adding, "More tea anyone?"

Siri dropped back into his classic and incredible old-time movie star voice. "I say, I have been trying for *years* to get that Shirley Temkin's voice down just so. It's tougher than you'd imagine to sound exactly like an eight-year-old girl."

The Henchman was about to agree when suddenly something began battering the outside of the DBP. A quick glance out the window showed it had begun to hail. Offering up the customary "What in tarnation?" Dutch looked from the cow to the impersonator.

Brad spoke up, the brown cow head on his shoulders masking his astonishment. "Oh, this is not good."

Within seconds, what had begun as an average, ordinary hailstorm with average, ordinary hailstones had changed. As the trio gazed out the window, the hailstone diameter increased in a matter of moments, from pea-sized, to peanut-sized, from quarter-sized to golf ball-sized. And while the hailstone size increased, so did the pounding sound on the hull of the RV. And once the golf ball-sized hail became grapefruit sized-hail, windshields in the newly converted sales lot began to shatter and huge dents formed all over the new and previously pristine trucks.

Suddenly, there was a flash of movement, and in an instant the famous bullfighter and his two-biker audience members dashed into the DBP.

The Henchman stared at the impossible storm and corresponding destruction outside, and then turned his attention to the three new refugees. They were completely drenched, but seemed unhurt.

Dutch looked at them and just had to shiver. Regrouping, he rapidly rubbed his hands together before asking determinedly, "Okay, who's up for some tea?"

ᘓᕽᘓᕽᘓᕽ

Once Caceres had installed most of the side slats and positioned the ramp onto the back of the long flatbed truck, Mrs. O'Leary gradually began to lead the small herd of cattle out of the barn and into the storm. She'd made one last ditch effort to lure John Steerman away from his whittling to help out, but the attempt seemed to have the opposite effect, as instead of helping load the beasts, he'd hopped up and headed into the house, without a parting word or even an imaginary hat tip.

Margaret had looked through the front window of the place to see what was so darned important, but all she could see was John plopping himself down into his easy chair and turning on some black and white movie. With a heavy sigh, Margaret had headed back to the barn.

And now animal loading began in earnest, and the first beast up was the bull, Beefy. His eyes were level with Mrs. O'Leary's and she got the feeling, as Beefy took a good, hard look at her, that the animal resented being disturbed during his afternoon nap. Once outside, though Margaret thought it was probably just her imagination, it seemed as though the bull's attitude changed from resentment to disdain – not a good transition in a sixteen hundred-pound animal. Still, Beefy offered up only a relatively benign "moo" when Margaret handed him off to Caceres, and no resistance at all as he was led up the ramp to the back of the flatbed. Once positioned up front toward the cab, the bull began to sniff the flowers Caceres had placed there.

The man swatted the animal on the rear end, adding a chastising, "No, Señor Beefy. No flowers for you." Beefy mooed in response and continued to sniff at the blossoms.

Next up in the evacuation process were the three small calves, Crackle, Curly and Huey. Margaret thought it best to position the youngsters between Dad and Mom, just to ensure they were as comfortable as could be. The little ones got to experience rain for the first time upon leaving the barn, as the region had been in an extreme drought since before they were born and there had not been a single wet day in the interim. One might think that such a new sensation would have impacted the three amigos at least in some manner, but they seemed not to notice and scampered right up the ramp to stand next to Dad. They were easy to tell apart, as Huey was jet black all over, Crackle was white as could be and Curly was a combination of the two and looked like a huge sandwich cookie.

The mother of the calves, dubbed Mrs. Beefy by the kindly Mrs. O'Leary, required extra attention to get loaded into the back of the flatbed. The gentle cow was hypersensitive to sunlight and, during the day, sported a custom-made red bandana eye shield. It was late afternoon by the time the herd was being loaded onto the truck and, even though the sky was clouded over and the sun was nowhere to be seen, the blinder needed to remain on or Mrs. Beefy would be in excruciating pain.

"There you go, Señora Beefy," Caceres encouraged the beast once she was handed to him. "Slowly, up the ramp now. Your little ones and large husband are there." The kind Caceres seemed to believe that the cow could actually understand what he was saying. He added, "And pay no attention to any flowers you may see. I mean smell, Mrs. Beefy."

She eventually was maneuvered into position where she nuzzled her calves. Moos rang out atop the flatbed. It was precious.

The next cow Mrs. O'Leary led out of the barn was her personal favorite. This one was what would typically be called a teenager, a rambunctious spotted brown cow named Lactose Tolerant. Lactose was a prodigious milk producer, even at her relatively young age. She had massive udders for a cow of her breed, though had gone through no type of special enhancement surgery to acquire them. Margaret liked Lactose Tolerant best because the cow was rowdy and reminded the woman of her earlier days. The cow would break the rules and an occasional law, and then would go into hiding as if she just knew she was going to be caught. Margaret O'Leary could relate to that. She could have sworn the cow winked at her as Caceres led her up the ramp. That didn't surprise her at all; she and Lactose Tolerant were kindred spirits.

The final three cows up the ramp were, like the calves, part of the same cow litter. They were sisters, and inseparable. Named Mollie, Morucha and Mewati, the cows were well-behaved and, in Margaret's opinion, rather boring. She once said to the three as a group, "You ladies have never done a daring thing in your lives." They couldn't deny the accusation; they were cows. But John Steerman adored them, and they spent all day chewing cud.

Only the trained eye could tell the three completely brown animals apart. Actually, only the trained ear could. Their respective moos were just a half a note off from one another, a difference most people couldn't hear. John Steerman, he of perfect pitch, could always tell. He just had to create clever means to get the girls to actually moo. But once he did it was party over. Their moos gave their identities away.

Caceres loaded the three cows up the ramp with relative ease and then lifted the rear slat into position, assuring no cow was in danger of falling out. He then tucked the ramp up under the bed. By the time he'd completed the task, John had reappeared on the porch of the farmhouse. He called Caceres over to him.

Margaret could see the two men discussing something, but couldn't make out what they were saying. The rain was still coming down in sheets and lightning continued to flash all around. The wind would whip up into a frenzy, die down for a bit and then start back up again. Caceres eventually nodded to John, and John handed him a set of keys and a slip of paper. Off Caceres sprinted, through the rain to the aard-vark-laden pickup. He started the vehicle and sped away down the now-muddy driveway toward the main gate. Margaret followed his progress until the truck was out of sight, and then was startled to find John Steerman standing right next to her.

He tipped his imaginary hat. "Ma'am."

"Where's he going?" she asked. "I thought I was going to drive the pickup."

John then spoke more words at once to Margaret O'Leary than he had ever spoken, unless you count Donny Duck quacks as words. (She again recalled his phenomenal imper-sonation back in elementary school.)

He began, "I will drive the flatbed. You come along. We need to get to safety."

He wasn't asking. He turned, walked up to the driver side door and climbed in. Still rather flummoxed, Margaret took a look through the flatbed slats to check on the animals. All nine of them were munching on flowers. She chuckled, thinking how proud she was of the three boring lookalike bovines. They were finally doing something daring.

Mrs. O'Leary tried to climb into the passenger side of the truck, no easy task for the woman. John sensed her difficulty and quickly got out and dashed around to her side of the rig. Giving her rear end an impressive push, he got the woman into position inside the cab.

Within minutes, the duo and their hefty cargo were bouncing through the storm down the driveway toward the main highway. Margaret reflected on the fact that they hadn't locked anything up or turned anything off; they'd just left. She was pretty sure a now-redundant sprinkler was on over near the toolshed. She wondered whether or not she had turned the coffee pot off in her shack, and knew for sure that all the lights were on in the main farmhouse – she could see them reflected in the passenger side window.

And, of all of the possibilities and probabilities Margaret O'Leary was considering as John turned onto Highway One, of things left turned on or, by chance, turned off, the one thing she never considered, or imagined for that matter, was the fact that, in about ten seconds, things were going to get really, really bad.

ᘓᘏ ᘓᘏ ᘓᘏ

Typhoons, hurricanes, cyclones and other sea-born storms can be incredibly destructive. Tornadoes and damaging hail are typically on the periphery of the true devastation, which is often credited to the wind and the storm surge. The latter of the two, the intrusion of the ocean on the land, was dynamically catastrophic in Typhoon Bessie, the appearance of which stunned emergency planners and weather forecasters alike. None of the so-called experts had predicted the sudden "grandmother-of-all-storms," as it was later dubbed. The call to seek shelter never went out, except from a lone policeman and his assistant deputy, who at least made an effort to get some folks to safety.

John Steerman had just turned north onto Highway One when the wall of water hit, surging over a small sea wall and across the road, slamming directly into the flatbed, jack-knifing the rig and sending it sliding on the sudden wave for a moment before it tipped over. It careened on its side for about thirty feet to the right of the road before crashing into a small rise off the shoulder of the highway. The truck came to rest with a loud crunching sound as it rammed into the rise, engine running and smoke pouring from the locked-up brakes on each wheel.

John's immediate concern was for Margaret, who was knocked unconscious during the crash. The woman was now below John in the cab of the rig, which now lay on its side.

Both of them were held in place by their seat belts. John was stunned but otherwise unhurt as he pushed the door next to him up and away into the rain. He had to figure out a way to get the good woman out of the wreckage.

He considered for a moment the well-being of the cows and flowers, the precious cargo he'd been tasked with getting to safety. It was raining too hard to see much of anything back behind the cab, the billowing smoke from the wheel wells further obscuring his vision. Once he'd climbed out of the cab section of the truck and dropped down, he splashed into a couple feet of water. He knew he had to get Mrs. O'Leary out of that cab, and scanned the water around him for something he could use as a rescue tool. In the fading and, as he noticed, purple-tinted light, he saw a piece of rope several feet long floating away. It was the lasso Caceres had used to guide the herd up the ramp and onto the flatbed. The man must have tossed the rope into the back of the truck once all the animals were loaded in. John sloshed a few feet from the truck and grabbed the rope before it could be carried out to sea. It was perfect for him to use to save the woman. He hopped back up to the open driver side door and took a look inside. Margaret O'Leary was beginning to stir.

All of the cows had been launched out of the flatbed when the storm surge hit, even the bull, Beefy. Each of them was still alive but, as with Mrs. O'Leary, the force of the accident had knocked them all unconscious. They ended up strewn about over a twenty-square-foot patch of what had been dry land, but what was now a couple feet of water. In the driving rain and intense wind, the herd was in definite peril. The animals were about to drown.

Their salvation, as it were, came from a most unlikely source: a purple, glowing pile of debris, carried across the ocean in the months since "The Incident" (another water-based disaster). The radioactive heap settled in amongst the cows, bobbing away innocently, as though the now-deadly Nucliette, access door gone, was not in the middle of the mangled mess. And as John Steerman was making progress in lifting Margaret O'Leary out of the wreckage of the cab, and as Typhoon Bessie bore down upon Bay City, the near-dead cows, all nine of them, began to mutate. As mutations go, the mutation of the cows was horrible indeed.

Officer Chris Holstein was feeling he and his new assistant deputy were making progress, but just not fast enough. It was beginning to get dark and he was afraid that the shops would close for the day and folks would head home on their own, without the opportunity to have been warned about the danger that was no doubt lurking. And the danger element was a huge part of the evacuation process, or so the policeman thought.

But there wasn't much he could do about that, and Holstein decided he and Assistant Deputy Chateaubriand would have to carry on as best they could. Whoever went home warned, well, that was a good thing. As for those folks who went home on their own without proper danger notification, well, those folks would just have to fend for themselves. Such is the nature of the job of evacuating people.

Ivory was warning folks in the businesses and on the street on the west side of Lineback, while Holstein handled the other side of the road. She dove right into the task at hand, and was quickly outpacing the officer. It took him some time to disengage his stun gun from the light fixture at the Calfeteria, plus he was slowed down a bit by his own politeness. He'd greet everyone and bow deeply in introduction before offering up the dire prediction. It caused unneeded delay, but Officer Holstein would simply have it no other way. Politeness, he felt, should never play second fiddle to anything, not even life-and-death situations. In fact, because the situation was so terrifying, he added an extra measure of kindness, and his bows were even deeper and more theatrical than usual.

So, by the time Chris Holstein had safely and efficiently evacuated three businesses on his side of the street, Ivory had done five. That relative pace continued as evening approached. Throughout it all, the rain, wind and frequent lightning continued unabated. Many shoppers headed home just to get out of the weather, and each time Holstein saw a car drive away, he hoped and prayed, literally getting down on his knees (which slowed him down all the more), that these people were leaving because they, in fact, had received a proper warning.

Holstein successfully got everyone out of the musical instrument store, Moore Cowbell, owned by kindly old Abigar Moore, retired teacher and rodeo clown. He had a tough time getting the message across at the two side-by-side restaurants, the Burger Joint and the Chicken Coop, both of which were owned by former reality television star, Asturian Mountain. (Mr. Mountain wasn't personally in either establishment at the time.) The officer had a tough time convincing the teen-aged assistant manager at one location and his identical twin, running the other, that this all wasn't some sort of huge practical joke. Holstein had to act as an intermediary between the two for a while, hopping back and forth between the Joint and the Coop, in an attempt to convince each of them that their respective twin was okay with the plan to get out and get out fast. The effort was exhausting to say the least, but the dedicated policeman would not be deterred. Once the officer succeeded in emptying both eateries, he continued down Lineback Street.

Across the road, Assistant Deputy Ivory Chateaubriand was suffering no fools. Any tarrying, be it by shopkeepers or shoppers, would simply not be tolerated. Ivory would enter a shop with purpose and dive right into her evacuation speech.

"Folks," she'd begin, "I know you all know me, but you don't know I am now a member of the Bay City Police Department."

And though she had no uniform, and sported no badge, people seemed to believe her.

They did know Ivory; she was a staple of Mashona Town. She spent big money in all the shops and, sunglass-encumbered coif notwithstanding, the woman was known by all to be forthright, honest and rich.

That greeting got the attention of most people, and she would continue, "As an official police assistant deputy, I am hereby closing this location. We have reliable information that a threat is imminent and may be coming up the hill right now. I need you all to leave in an orderly fashion. Get to your homes and lock your doors."

For a good percentage of the shoppers, that was all the convincing they'd need. Without questioning further, they'd simply set down whatever items they may have had gathered up and head out the door into the storm. Most of the shopkeepers did the same, just leaving the premises without hesitation, leaving lights on and doors unlocked. A few of the business owners weren't so fast to evacuate and needed some convincing to get a move on. And, unlike back in the Calfeteria, no dramatics, no chair-standing and no fool-calling was needed. Of course, Ivory had given Officer Holstein back his stun gun. The gun sort of was the attention-getter back at the diner.

Ivory figured that having no gun and no handcuffs would only improve her fledgling policing skills. She had no clue how long her recent deputizing might be in effect, but she was beginning to like it. Perhaps, she thought, she would be interested in becoming a one- or two-hour-a-day police officer once all of the evacuating was done.

One shop owner in particular required additional convincing to leave the area and head to safety. Sir Sanga Loin owned the Blade Barn, a store that sold a wide array of knives, blades and even swords. Sir Loin fancied himself quite the swordsman, having once qualified for the Olympic Games representing the tiny Polynesian country of Butana, where he had been born. And, though he never actually made it to the competition because of a horrifying bicycle accident in which he was T-boned by a runaway milk cart, the man ended up being knighted because he'd become such a local celebrity.

His shop was devoid of customers when the new law enforcer entered. She went through her evacuation proclamation protocol.

The shopkeeper shook his head. "I can't just leave my hardware behind."

"Most folks aren't doing it, but you could just lock the doors on your way out," she countered. "You do have an alarm or something, don't you? Either way, you need to get home now."

"That's just it, Mrs. Chateaubriand," Loin continued. "I don't have a home. I live here. I sleep in the back."

That was something the assistant deputy hadn't anticipated. She considered options for a bit, and then asked, "Well, do you at least have locks on this place? I mean, you *can* lock up, can't you?"

The man replied, "Yes, of course. I lock up every evening."

Ivory dug into her pocket and pulled out a set of keys. She handed them to Sir Loin.

"Okay, here's what I want you to do," she said decisively. "You're going to my place so you can be safe. I live in Mashona, over on Criollo, by Braford. It's the big white house with the orange picket fence. You can't miss it. It's right across the street from the Rock House."

The Rock House was the most popular steakhouse in Bay City, primarily because of the view. Located at the north end of the Mashona neighborhood, just west of the infamous switchbacks, the restaurant sat perched right on the edge of the Bay City plateau, and faced both the ocean to the west and the bay to the north. Jutting out over the rocks down below and perched atop giant pilings that held the building up, the Rock House offered an amazing vista of the Big Bridge, the wondrous golden suspension bridge that led across the bay and into North Bay City.

Ivory continued, "You can lock up here and head over to my house. At least then I know you'll be safe."

Sir Sanga Loin thought for a bit, wondering how two blocks would make any difference in the overall safety of things, but shrugged it off, figuring it was about time to close up for the day anyway. He nodded and, keys in hand, stepped around the counter, ready to follow any further directions Ivory had for him.

Within a few minutes, Ivory was back outside, the retail establishment locked tightly up and its proprietor headed to the relative safety of the Chateaubriand abode. She scanned Lineback Street, squinting hard to make out details through the driving rain. To her right, through the gloaming and the downpour, she could make out the outline of Canchim Tower, still a block and a half away. And, across the street and to her left, she could see Officer Holstein, out on the sidewalk in front of the two identical-looking fast food restaurants. The officer appeared to be chatting with twin teenagers. He offered them up a full and wondrous bow, and the youngsters scampered through the rain to a nearby Tauros.

The center of Lineback Street had become a small river, and odds and ends and assorted papers flowed back down toward the switchbacks.

"This is getting worse," Ivory lamented.

A hobbyhorse and a bobblehead doll floated by. Ivory put her head down and trudged into the storm toward the next business, the appliance store appropriately named Home on the Range.

"It's getting late," she thought. *"I have got to get moving."*

🐂 🐂 🐂

Five men sat around the picnic table inside the gigantic Tauros RV. The Henchman, mascot and impersonator had been joined by the two now-dried bikers. The bullfighter was in front of the full-length mirror at the back of the DBP, practicing his cape swishing.

Initially the bikers had introduced themselves as Big Dog and Stinky, but after a bit a level of trust was established between the two and their new companions, aided no doubt by the phenomenal relaxation tea The Henchman had served up for one and all. Big Dog (and he wasn't that large of a man) admitted to being a baker from the Financial District of Bay City. His real name was Hanwoo Istoben. His friends called him Han. It was the rest of the Horro bikers who had dubbed him Big Dog. He really wasn't sure why. Han was continually and nervously applying lip balm, as if it would calm him beyond what the tea could do.

He again wiped his lips with the tiny stick of balm and then offered it up to his new friends. "Lip balm, anyone?" he asked.

The man first introduced as Stinky shook his head. He was an accountant from the Mashona neighborhood whose real name was Randall Shorthorn. But his friends didn't call him Randy, they called him Shorty, though he was well over six feet tall. The Horros had named him Stinky, an odd nickname for a guy whose odor was the same as any other guy, biker or not. After some discussion, everyone agreed to call the two men Han and Shorty, since they were all becoming friends.

"Why are you always offering people your lip balm, Han? It's gross." Shorty did look quite disgusted.

"I'm just nervous, I guess," Han replied. "You know what they say, 'Keep balm and carry on.'" Han smiled.

"Who says that? Nobody says that." Then, to the others, Shorty continued. "Watch out, once Han gets on a roll with his so-called 'wise sayings,' there's no stopping him."

That got Dutch's attention. He chimed in, "Oh, I love wise sayings, do some more!"

Shorty shook his head again and laughed. "You asked for it," he said.

Han went on. "Well, here's one for you. My grandparents had a coffee urn that they placed on their fireplace mantle. Whenever they had loose change, they'd toss it in the urn. Gramps would always tell me that 'a penny saved is a penny urned.'" Han smiled.

Shorty groaned.

Dutch, who had been getting himself some more tea, stopped mid-refill, set down the teakettle so he could have access to both hands, and applauded.

Siri Batangas offered up, in character of course, a cheery, "Well done, chap."

Brad, still in his cow mascot outfit, pumped a cow arm, smiled inside the cow head and said, "Awesome!"

"And, of course, there is this one..."

Han was ready to continue, but then Salers Salorn approached from the rear of the RV.

All eyes turned to the bullfighter who said knowingly, "The hell storm. She stopped."

Indeed, the tremendous pounding of ice had ceased. They all took a look out the window. The rain had stopped and a small patch of blue sky could be seen in amongst the angry clouds.

"Well," Dutch offered up, "We'd best go assess the damage and see if anyone's hurt." He put down his teacup and headed for the door. The five others followed him outside.

There was not a single truck left undamaged by the freak hailstorm. Most had shattered windshields, and those that didn't had hoods that looked like they'd just been battered for a half an hour by grapefruit-sized hailstones, which, of course, they had. A few of the rigs had flat tires, and more than one had accumulated a pile of ice balls in the bed. As for the rest of the gigantic orbs, they were scattered about everywhere, and the sextet had to stomp through them as they made their way back around to the front of the arena. There were no other people, be it Brain Truster, biker or random other person, to be seen in the truck section of the lot.

The devastation was even worse around the front of the building, as in this area cars were smashed beyond recognition, lying in twisted wrecks on top of each other. Clearly something more, and far worse, than a simple enormous freak hailstorm had occurred here. It looked as though someone or something had tossed the more than forty vehicles randomly about, letting them fall as they may. Yes, there were the remnants of the gigantic ice balls here, but what happened in the front of the Cow Palace was much, much more catastrophic than just a few hundred feet away, where the shelter of the RV had been such a lifesaver.

"What the heck?" Dutch asked aloud, scanning the wreckage in disbelief.

There was a tap on his left shoulder. He turned his head to see a hoof doing the tapping. Dutch didn't know whether to laugh, cry or scream.

"Mr. Friesian. Does this mean the car sale is over?" It was the mascot, Brad.

Dutch sighed. "I'd say so, Brad."

The cow head nodded. "Um, do we still get paid?" he asked.

"I don't know, Brad," the despondent The Henchman replied. "I don't know."

Dutch took another look around the ruins. This time he noticed that most of the motorbikes were gone. They weren't in the wreckage, they were just gone, save for the three parked under the entryway awning next to Red's unscathed Cattle-ac. The bikes that were left belonged to Han, Shorty and the Horro leader, Pajuna. The sight of the oversized car brought Dutch out of his devastation daze.

"Where is everyone?" he asked. "Where could they be?"

His question seemed to inspire the little band to get moving. Brad shrugged, his cow shoulders hopping up a bit. The bullfighter headed into the car carnage, swishing his cape from side to side as he assessed the situation. Han and Shorty headed to their cycles to make sure they were undamaged.

It was the impersonator who replied to the query. He opted for a Southern accent and vernacular reminiscent of a past president of the country. "Let me answerify your questionification," he said.

"This guy is good!" Dutch thought.

Siri continued. "The bikers are gone. They've done vamoosed. My guess is, anyone left ducked inside that big building over there." He pointed to the front entryway of the arena, where the two bikers were each kneeling, closely examining their rides.

The Henchman turned and sprinted toward the front entry. "Come on, let's see," he called out to Siri.

The man broke into a trot after Dutch.

The duo jogged past the bikers and up to the front doors. Dutch pulled on the first door they came to, but it was locked.

"Try another," Siri instructed.

The second was locked too. With Siri's help, they tugged on all fourteen of the arena's main entry doors. They were all locked. The two shaded their eyes and tried to peer through a small side window and into the arena. It was completely dark. All Dutch could make out was the outline of a picnic table.

"What the hell is going on?" Dutch asked.

Siri Batangas replied, this time sounding a bit scared but not sounding like anyone famous, "What the hell, indeed."

$$\text{🐂 🐂 🐂}$$

Despite the fact water was gushing into the basement from the stairway at the Floral and Dance Sciences building, the large area of the room ensured the level of that water rose at a fairly slow rate. Dr. Herens and Devon assessed the situation, and the student used some charts he had back at his cubicle to estimate they had three hours and twenty-four minutes before they'd be in serious danger. Basement Fillage Rates, or BFRs as Devon called them, were one of the key factors in determining the financial impact weather had on the economy, particularly since the computer server room for most every stock exchange in the country is located in a basement somewhere. And water and servers don't mix.

Herens recommended they first try to find additional lighting, as Devon's emergency device simply did not give off enough light for them to attempt any sort of meaningful escape. As luck would have it, the basement of the building was used to store all sorts of supplies, inventory and the odd experiment or two from AAU's diverse assortment of not only unusual combination majors, but also student activity groups. A few cubicles away from where Devon did his research was the cubicle-home of the Ravy Wavy Light Stick Surfers, a group of students who had moved their wildly popular "rave" parties out into the ocean. The cubicle had quite a stash of both light sticks and surfing gear. The light sticks – the type that, once snapped in the middle, gives off a modest green glow – immediately came in handy. The club had a case of them on a desk located right next to a brightly colored boogie board. Devon and the doc spent the next several minutes snapping and placing the light sticks throughout the basement, sloshing through the few inches of water and positioning the glowing sticks on the tops of the cubicle partition walls, about five feet up from the floor. Now at least the two could see and get a much better grasp of the situation at hand. Student and professor both hoped they wouldn't need the actual board from the cubicle, but both secretly felt better knowing it was there.

Though there were assorted closets around the perimeter of the basement, there most assuredly was no way out other than the elevator or the stairs. Devon's prediction of a massive storm was spot on and the young man pointed out to Professor Herens that the water now accumulating in the basement was seawater, no doubt from the storm surge created by the typhoon.

"We might be the lucky ones, Professor Herens," Devon explained. "Anyone at street level would have been swept away by the surge. I mean, we are just a few hundred feet from the ocean."

The professor shook his head, knowing Devon was correct. The thing that drew so many kids to AAU was that it was situated right next to the Pacific. And it was this very fact that now made the campus so vulnerable. He could only imagine the devastation above.

"Devon," he said. "We have just got to find a way out of here. People may need our help."

The student nodded in agreement. They had both tried several times to make it up the stairs, but the rushing water was too intense.

Devon replied, "You're right, Professor. Nobody even knows we are down here, so we're on our own. And I'm thinking the only way out is up and through that elevator shaft."

Dr. Herens looked over at the closed elevator. "Maybe together we can pry that door open and then shimmy up." Devon looked dubious, though a little less so after the professor added, "We only need to climb one floor."

The determined duo headed over to the elevator but, try as they might, they could not get the door to budge. It was tough getting any leverage; there was just nothing to grab on to. So, Devon got down low, the professor stood tall, and they pushed on the door in an attempt to get it to slide. After a few minutes, they stepped away, thoroughly stumped by the mystery of the elevator door.

The professor rubbed his chin. "That's weird," he said. "Usually these things are meant to be opened by hand."

"Yeah, it seems like the door is locked for some reason," Devon agreed. "Maybe we can find some sort of wedge. I don't see a keyhole anywhere."

And, for certain, there was no keyhole to be found. So about the basement the professor and his student slogged, looking for anything they might be able to find to pry open the door. The light from the dozens of glow sticks was adequate but by no means surgery room-bright. They stuck close to one another and searched as a team, going cubicle by cubicle throughout the room.

Many of the spaces were empty, but in a few they did find some items of interest. AAU offered a major in tropical veganology, which is the study of the effort to convert the carnivorous fauna of the countries on or near the equator into herbivores. One cubicle was clearly the office space for the single student pursuing that major, and in addition to assorted nets and cookbooks there was a fifty-gallon tank teeming with piranha fish.

"Gosh I hope those don't get loose," the professor said, only slightly joking.

Devon wondered if these fish were actual vegans yet, or simply vegans-in-training. There were several bags of carrots next to the tank. He also wondered, with a shudder, how long these guys could survive in salt water.

Not too far away, the campus society known as the Student Union for Cutlery Knowledge occupied a couple of cubicles. Several types of cleavers, butcher knives and those amazing Oriental knives sold on TV were on display in a small glass case.

Devon looked admiringly at the knife that could cut a penny in half. "I was a member of SUCK when I was a freshman," he said wistfully. "We had a lot of fun. I miss those guys."

The professor, who was only half-listening because he'd just caught sight of what he hoped would be their salvation, asked, "How's that?" but quickly changed the subject. "Over here. Look, Devon. This could do the trick."

Directly across from the dual SUCK cubicles was the space used by the university student who was studying timberology. The professor had spoken briefly to the young lady who was pursuing the degree. They'd chatted in the very same elevator that was now causing such a problem. The professor had asked her about her major and she said she was studying third-century timber companies and the impact that the beaver pelt trade had on the industry. And though at the time the professor thought he may have found the most worthless of all of AAU's goofy degrees, at present he couldn't have been happier that such a degree existed. There on a desk in the cubicle, next to the photos of beaver pelts and beaver dams, propped up against a stack of thick books about the history of chopping down trees, were the exact two items needed to get the elevator door open: a sledge hammer and a woodsplitting maul.

"What are the odds?" the professor queried.

"I can figure that out, I'm sure," Devon boasted, picking up both of the tools.

Typically, a woodsplitting maul is positioned on a freshly cut log, resting in a split in the wood that is almost always, for some reason, there. An axe-wielder takes a massive swing with the intention of bringing the back of the axe down onto the maul. At that point either the piece of wood splits, or the axe head misses the maul entirely and slams into the leg of the axe-wielder, often with painful results.

Having a sledge hammer available was fortuitous, and was a much safer option than having to use an axe. This particular tool was a small one, just about twice the size of the average hammer found in a carpenter's toolbox.

Back at the elevator, the professor offered to hold the tapered maul in position at the left edge of the door, right at swing level for Devon, just at the seam between the door and the frame. He assessed the situation. The water in the room was now above his ankles, and it was cold.

"This had better work," thought Dr. Herens.

"Okay, Devon. Try not to miss." The professor held the maul steady and closed his eyes.

Devon said, "Okay, here goes nothing."

He took a mighty swing, a direct hit on the maul. They both looked. Nothing. The door was still closed tight.

"Try it again, Devon," the professor offered. "Give it all you've got."

The student took another swing, grunting ferociously as he brought the hammer onto the maul with a loud "THWACK."

Whether the elevator door was locked or jammed, the two gentlemen would never find out. With the latest swing, the door slid slightly to the right, split apart from the frame by a fraction of an inch. And from between that smallest of spaces came a trickle of water.

This was not good. The men looked at one another, panic-stricken.

Professor Herens grabbed his student by the arm, turned and began to shout, "Devon, let's get--"

Just then, with a horrible "WHOOSH," the elevator door flew open and a torrent of water slammed into the room. In an instant, Devon and the professor were both knocked off their feet and carried back toward the cubicles. In the sudden rapids, both fought to keep their heads above the wave, smashing into chairs, laptops and assorted office parapher-nalia. They were tumbled nearly all the way to the wall at the far end of the room, where they finally could gather themselves enough to grip on to one another and the boogie board, which had also been tossed to the back of the room in the flood.

"Are you okay, Professor?" Devon asked once he'd regrouped.

Dr. Herens had swallowed some of the seawater and was looking a bit green, although that could have been the glow given off by the light sticks that remained atop the cubicle walls in this section of the room. The rest of them had been knocked about in the inundation and were floating around the room in the knee-high water.

Instead of water only flowing down the stairs, it was also now gushing out from the elevator shaft. Things had turned dire in a hurry.

"Devon," the professor said. "What say we climb up on these desks so we can get out of the water? And grab that board. I think we're going to need it."

"Good idea, Dr. Herens," the student replied. "This water is cold!"

But it wasn't the temperature that had the professor so worried about getting out of the water. It was the fish. While being rolled along in the flash flood, he'd seen the piranha tank floating by. It was empty.

Most people spend very little time considering cows. Those who do often think of them only when mulling over the type of milk or cheese to purchase at the local grocery store, or perhaps when deciding on the type of steak they wish to order at a fancy restaurant. Otherwise, most folks just don't give cows much thought.

Certainly, as the popularity of the cow mascot illustrates, cows in general are thought of as entertaining, if not hilarious, creatures. But only some would call the animals cute, even the youngest of the species. Few, if any, children would prefer a calf as a pet to a kitten, bunny or puppy. Even the other farm animal babies – foals, chicks and lambs – are considered by most people to be much more adorable than calves.

While it is rare to find someone who would call cows, or even a calf, cute, it is still possible. But there could be no one who would confuse the newly mutated calves, Huey, Crackle and Curly, with any precious baby animal, like an adorable baby duck. Or anything adorable for that matter.

The three sprung to their hooves in unison once the radio-active soup had run through their bodies. Mutation affected each of the trio in exactly the same way. All three now sported sharp, jagged teeth, with mouths that looked eerily similar to that of the reclusive Blue Albion shark. It also seemed as though someone had given the youngsters hefty doses of the popular Green Bull energy drink, as they ran everywhere.

They each had glowing, purple eyes. They sniffed around like dachshunds on the trail of a frightened mole, darting from truck tire to signpost to one of the metal doors from the debris pile, bashing into one another and anything else that happened to be in the way. Adjacent to that metal door, wrapped up in the flypaper, seaweed and some fishing net that had glommed on during the trip across the ocean, was a long-dead coloursided white back fish. Once Huey bumped into that and determined it was edible, he started tearing into it, fish pieces flying everywhere. Crackle and Curly were on it in seconds and within a minute all that was left was the white back's skeleton. That sent the three calves (if that's what they could still be called) careening off, madly searching for more food. They sniffed at, but thankfully didn't attempt to chomp into, the rest of the herd.

Lactose Tolerant was the next cow to regain consciousness. She got to her hooves and then climbed up the embankment next to the demolished truck and began munching on some grass she found up there. Like the youngsters, Lactose now had glowing, purple eyes. She looked unaffected by both the accident and the radiation, except for one major change: the udders. Lactose Tolerant's massive udders had moved. The bags had grown impossibly big and had traveled from under the beast up to her sides. It looked as though she was wearing overstuffed saddlebags. From one of the teats on her right side, a few drops of green liquid leaked out and fell into the patch of grass. The area the drops hit sizzled and burned, the blades there vaporized by the acidy concoction spilled from the udder above.

At about the time the grass was being concurrently eaten and acidified, Mrs. Beefy slowly climbed to her feet. Still donning the red bandana eye shield, from behind which a purple glow emanated, the cow looked about as if assessing her current situation, and then made a beeline straight for the ocean. She hobbled significantly, as though a front leg may have been injured. She moved across the highway, made her way over a side rail and dropped down into the eight feet of water that now covered the beach. Once in the water, Mrs. Beefy let out a loud "MOO" and began, incredibly, to swim. The mutated bovine would dive completely underwater for a few seconds, pop back up and do an unbelievable assortment of what appeared to be breaststrokes, sidestrokes and even backstrokes. She paid no attention to her three calves and just splashed around in the ocean. And, considering her size, some of the splashes were quite impressive.

While Mrs. Beefy paddled about offshore, one of the three sibling dairy cows, Mewati, came to. She was horrific to look at, as a ridge of vertical scales had sprouted up along her spine and through her hide. The beast's hairy tail had transformed into something resembling threaded metal ropes, akin to the cables that hold up an elevator. And, below her now-purple eyes, steam flowed out of her nostrils, as if foreshadowing something more terrible. Mewati seemed disoriented upon waking and began stumbling away from the wreckage, back toward the front gate of Contented Corners.

The bull, Beefy, was the next of the herd to come to consciousness. Other than his piercing purple eyes, the only thing that seemed to mutate in Beefy were his horns. Normally extending out about a foot and a half on either side of his head, these radiated horns had moved to the very front of the bull and had quadrupled in size, each stretching a full six feet. And now, a circle of incredibly sharp smaller horns protruded out from his ankles, just above each hoof. Once Beefy hopped out of the roadside pond into which he'd been tossed, the bull strode out into the middle of the road and paused, as if assessing the situation.

His mate was mooing and swimming in the ocean. Lactose Tolerant was up on a rise to his left, chewing on some grass. His three young ones were bouncing about like insane pinballs, snarling and ripping apart whatever they considered to be food. Mewati was walking in a wobbly fashion back down the highway, in the direction from which they had come. Turning around, Beefy saw the flatbed on its side, with John Steerman positioned over the open driver side door, looking down into the cab. He was doing something, but exactly what the bull could not be sure. That left two more cows – Mollie and Morucha – unaccounted for. But as the bull scanned the pool, he could see only one quite large animal stirring next to the pile of debris, which was giving off a faint, purple glow.

Through it all – the mutations, the awakenings and the cab-side rescue – the typhoon raged on. The initial storm surge was, Beefy could sense, the first of many to come.

And that was another feature of the bull's mutation. Beefy, amazingly, had become self-aware. He knew there was a storm raging. He knew how many animals were in his herd. He knew about the people who had cared for him before his recent evolution. He knew and could understand English. He knew and could understand Cow. And, though he didn't know how he knew, he knew another strong wave was imminent and he needed to get his herd to safety.

While Beefy was coming to the realization of things, the last two cows came to their senses. Or, more accurately, they came to their sense. In the most horrible and incredible transformation of all, the dairy cows, Mollie and Morucha, had morphed, combined, if you will, into one enormous animal. Far beyond any cow seen in one of those world record books or at a state fair, the new combination cow was about the size of an elephant. A big elephant. From the jungle.

It still had the proportional dimensions of a regular-sized cow, it was just enormous. And other than its outrageous size and purple eyes, it didn't seem as though anything else had changed on the animal.

MOLLIE AND MORUCHA, I SEE YOU ARE NOW ONE COW, thought the intelligent bull. *I SHALL CALL YOU KENANA, AND NOW WE ALL NEED TO LEAVE.*

☙☙☙

At that moment, John Steerman finally was able to hoist the much-relieved Mrs. O'Leary up out of the cab. The two climbed out and rested on the open door. Beefy was directly in front of them, horribly changed. Assorted other cows were scattered and skittering about, one of them impossibly enormous.

"Oh my," Margaret exclaimed. "What happened here?"

John just stared in disbelief.

Then Beefy began to moo, initially so low in tone the ground simply shook, then ascending to a more traditional, yet extra loud and extended, "MOOOOOO."

All the other cows, including Mrs. Beefy out in the water, stopped and looked directly at the bull. They were paying attention.

And still the mooing continued, rising in both octave and decibel level. John and Margaret had to cover their ears, both shutting their eyes tightly as if it would help keep out the sound. A horrible sound it was, now morphing away from a moo and into more of a wail. And from a wail the sound changed again to a primordial, flesh-rending, life-ending scream. The front windshield of the flatbed exploded, further startling the pair perched precariously on its side door. After thirty seconds or so, Beefy's howl subsided.

Before either John or Margaret could speak, all the cattle took off. Lactose Tolerant leapt from her grassy knoll to a spot on the truck right next to the terrified couple, then hopped off again, landing with a thud next to Beefy, who had turned and was heading up the highway toward Bay City. The three mutated calves came scurrying behind, dashing to and fro, snarling as they chased after their father. Mewati had turned around and was running next to the gigantic Kenana, small flames spurting out of her nostrils. The two mooed in perfect harmony as they passed John and Margaret. And, out in the surf, Mrs. Beefy followed, parallel to the others, swimming with amazing speed and precision through the roiling sea.

Once the herd had stampeded out of sight, John carefully guided Mrs. O'Leary down off of the capsized rig. They had a tough time fathoming all that had just occurred. After a quick look around, they stood silently at the back end of the flatbed and watched as the debris pile at the back of the truck flashed a faint purple light for a few moments and then went dark. The Nucliette was now dead, its damage done.

"Well, dang." John exclaimed. (That was practically obscene talk from the cowboy.)

"Was Mrs. Beefy swimming in the ocean?" Margaret asked. "Did I really see that?"

John replied simply, "Ma'am." The farmer was so out of sorts he didn't even try to tip his non-existent hat.

"Well, we can't just stay here, John." Mrs. O'Leary was insistent. "It'll be dark soon."

It was then the woman noticed a bright, red glow coming from Contented Corners. It was as if the entire farm was being lit by a gigantic, flickering flashlight. John saw it too and immediately started back down the highway toward the front gate.

"No, John." Margaret grabbed him by the arm. "I'll see to this. You have got to get your herd. They're headed up toward the city. And they're not normal, John. You need to hurry."

Steerman thought about his options, none of which were good. But at least now he figured he had only one course of action: get his cows. He offered up another "Ma'am," even throwing in the accompanying phantom hat tip, changed his course and headed back toward the truck. He grabbed the rope lasso he'd used to pull Margaret out of the cab, threw it over his right shoulder and broke into a sprint after the runaway herd.

Margaret felt relieved that John had done the hat tip before leaving. It meant to her that he was of a right mind. She sighed deeply, pulled her drenched rain slicker as tight as she could around her, then started off through the storm toward the main gate. She could tell right away what the problem was: Contented Corners was on fire.

🐂🐂🐂

"What do you mean you quit?" Officer Holstein asked. "You can't quit! We're not done warning everybody."

Ivory Chateaubriand was soaked to the bone. She was cold and tired, and didn't see the point in finishing up the evacuation process. Things had been so promising. Ivory had cleared out more than a dozen shops. But, just over halfway through her assigned route, Ivory had taken a nasty spill leaving the Lariat, the lone bar in Mashona Town. She'd turned down the sidewalk to head to the next business when a wind-blown runaway shopping cart from the Ayrshire Market, which she had cleared out a half an hour earlier, smacked into her behind. She was shoved forward, lost her balance and tripped off of the curb, falling to her knees down into the river rushing along Lineback Street. And though the water was only a few inches deep, it was enough to thoroughly douse the woman in murk. While she'd managed to avoid being hit by any of the various oddities being carried along in the torrent, the soon-to-be former assistant deputy had lost three pair of her favorite hair-top sunglasses in the spill. That was the proverbial last straw, and once she regained her footing, Ivory Chateaubriand had slogged across the roadway and made her way back to Officer Holstein. She was done.

"Look, I appreciate the deputizing and all, but I just want to go home and take a hot bath." Ivory explained. "Besides, most everyone has gone home. The bar was probably the last place open. It's dark, it's cold and I'm soaked."

"Assistant Deputy Chateaubriand," Holstein responded. "I know it looks like most people have left, but what if they haven't? What if there is a child or an elderly person in need of assistance?"

"Officer Holstein," Ivory said, "I am an elderly person in need of assistance."

The kindly officer hadn't considered that possibility. A sudden wave of compassion washed over him. His eyes softened and he reached out and took hold of Ivory's left hand. "Come, my good woman. I have an idea."

He led Ivory back past the shoe store called Hoofin' It to the Galloway House of Leather. The lights were on and the front door unlocked. It was warm and smelled nice inside. It had a comforting, westerny aroma. Galloway's sold all things leather, from sofas to hats and belts to all kinds of cozy, comfortable clothing. Mrs. Chateaubriand always enjoyed shopping at Galloway's and loved the wonderful atmosphere in the place, but was a bit confused as to why the officer had brought her into the store.

"I just want to go home," she lamented.

"I understand, Mrs. Chateaubriand, and of course I accept your resignation. I thank you immensely for the assistance you have provided this day." Officer Holstein bowed deeply, almost reverently. He continued, "You can rest assured I will do everything in my power to ensure you receive public commendation and perhaps even a key to Bay City from our mayor."

While Ivory appreciated the kindness offered up by Officer Holstein, the fact was she was still soaked. She stared at the officer helplessly, looking a bit like a drowned rat.

Internally chastising himself for his continued inability to properly care for the woman, Holstein took action. He looked about and darted over to a display rack several feet away. He grabbed a handful of chamois towels, dashed back and handed them to Ivory.

She took them from him, with no small amount of confusion crossing her countenance. "Officer?" she asked.

He explained. "Look, these things soak up water like crazy. You can't walk home from here, not in this weather and in your condition. So, let's at least get you dry and in some different attire, and I will escort you to your residence. Grab whatever clothes you want off the racks here, and head back to the dressing rooms. I will try to round us up something hot to drink. Does that sound okay?"

Ivory Chateaubriand then began to cry, Officer Holstein's kindness completely disarming her.

He gave the woman a reassuring hug, holding her while she sobbed. "There, there," he said softly, gently patting her shoulder. They embraced for a bit until she had calmed down to the point of being able to run the leather towel through her sopping hair.

"These things *are* amazing," she said.

After just a few seconds of dabbing, her locks and remaining sunglasses were practically completely dry.

Holstein could assess that the situation and Ivory had both stabilized. "I'm off then," he said, again bowing deeply. "Take anything you want to wear," he added, heading for the door. "I'll fix things later with Mr. Galloway."

Ivory moved toward the clothing section of the store while Officer Holstein ventured out into the darkness and the driving rain.

Ten minutes later, the policeman returned, two tall, steaming hot chocolates and a bag of food in hand. While he had found the Burger Joint locked tight, the Chicken Coop next door was not. The lights had been left on and all of the restaurant appliances were powered up. Holstein helped himself to a couple of the piping hot beverages and bagged up several chicken pieces from the warming oven. He dashed back into the leather store and set the food down on a counter next to one of the cash registers.

Ivory Chateaubriand was just coming out from one of the dressing rooms. She was quite a sight, with fancy brown cowboy boots and jet-black leather pants. She'd also chosen a white leather belt that featured a huge silver buckle with the engraved image of a longhorn steer. She'd managed to find a plaid, long sleeve flannel shirt. (Not everything sold in the shop was made of leather; just most everything.) Outside of the shirt, Ivory sported a retro cowboy-style leather jacket, replete with fringe dropping down from each arm.

Officer Holstein took the full measure of the woman, bowed deeply and said, "Howdy, Mrs. Chateaubriand."

Ivory blushed. "Oh, come on, Officer. I must look a fright. At least I'm dry and not so darned cold."

"Quite the contrary," Holstein replied. "You look wonderful. And check this out," he added, pointing to the hot chocolate and chicken. "I found us some food."

They both smiled. She headed over to the register and they dove into their small repast.

After eating in silence for a few minutes, Ivory spoke up. "Can I ask you a question, Officer Holstein?"

He responded, "After all we've been through, please call me Chris."

"That's sort of what I wanted to ask you," she said.

A look of confusion swept over the policeman.

Ivory clarified. "What I mean is, can you not call me Mrs. Chateaubriand again?"

"Certainly, Ivory," Chris replied.

"No, no. Can you please call me Assistant Deputy Chateaubriand? I'd like to rescind my resignation."

Clearly the drying off, new clothes and hot food had done the trick. Ivory Chateaubriand had returned to her old new self: the confident and capable newly appointed assistant deputy.

"Of course, Assistant Deputy Chateaubriand," Holstein said with a wide smile.

"Let's go finish our job, Officer Holstein," Ivory said. "We may have children and elderly persons in need of assistance."

"Agreed," Holstein responded. "But let's stick together. It's too dark, too dangerous and you don't have a radio. But just in case, here, you take mine." He handed Ivory his two-way.

"Oh-*kaaay*..." she said, uncertain about the logic behind such a decision.

Within minutes they were back on the sidewalk, headed south toward Canchim Tower. Next up was a shop called Florida Cracker, a place that featured all sorts of handmade, one-of-a-kind nutcrackers. The place still had its lights on and the purveyor of the shop could be seen dusting off some of the inventory toward the back of the store.

But, just before the two civil servants turned into the shop, they were distracted by a sloshing noise emanating from the middle of Lineback Street as if something large, or several things large, were wading through the road river. The noise was getting louder, and louder fast. Whatever it was, it was rapidly approaching the two, heading straight at them from the direction of the tower.

Instinctively, Officer Holstein put his right hand down to the holster at his hip, grabbing hold of his department-issued stun gun. Ivory wasn't sure what to do, so she held up the two-way she'd just been handed, ready to place a call if need be.

After a few tense moments, Holstein and Ivory could make out what appeared to be pinpricks of light; small purple dots. There were more than a dozen of them, coming directly at the pair. They were little and non-descript at first, but as the sound increased in loudness, the purple pinpricks expanded in size, bobbing up and down a bit, almost in conjunction with the amplifying sloshing sound.

"Oh my," Ivory whispered to the policeman. "I know what those are. Those are eyes."

Officer Holstein dropped the cup of hot chocolate he'd been holding in his left hand.

"Not only that," he agreed, "they're purple."

⊬⊱⊬⊱⊬

"It's not gonna work," The Henchman predicted. "The car won't go fast enough."

"We don't have any better ideas, so let's just let the cow try. It was his idea anyway."

Han had a point. He and Shorty had circumnavigated the entire arena, and had found neither an unlocked door nor a window that was down low enough or big enough for them to smash open and then climb into. They all decided that if they were going to rescue any survivors inside the building, their best chance would be to somehow break through the main entry doors.

The hailstorm refugees had all pulled on each of the fourteen doors in an attempt to get into the arena and after a bit of head scratching and some considerable mulling, Brad the mascot, still in full cow regalia (minus the head, which now sat in the middle row of the Cattle-ac), had hopped into the driver's seat of the oversized Tauros and called out excitedly, "Step aside, I'll drive through 'em!"

The mascot was apparently unaware that the vehicle's top speed was about two miles per hour. And now, with the group standing off at a safe distance, and the skeptical The Henchman shaking his head, Brad headed toward the metal entry doors at a pace just slightly faster than that of a steamroller. After about thirty seconds, the gigantic Tauros lightly tapped a few of the doors. Even the grill-mounted horns did no damage. The Henchman was right; the car couldn't generate enough speed to break through a strip of crepe paper, let alone the sturdy doors of the arena.

Brad the mascot snapped. He grabbed the cow head and hopped out of the Cattle-ac.

With a beet-red face, he jumped up and down, screaming and spitting, "No, no, no, no, no!"

The rest of the group each took a step back. The headless cow mascot reared back and hurled his cow head at one of the doors. It bounced harmlessly away.

"Damn you, Cow Palace!" Brad cursed.

He ran over, grabbed the head and gave it another heave. Again, it bounced away. He yelled another epithet, scrambled after the head again and was ready to re-launch when a sturdy hand grabbed his throwing arm. Brad spun around. It was the bullfighter.

Salers spoke up. "Stop, cow man. You crazy."

Brad stared hard at the Spanish European.

"Cow man, you crazy," Salers repeated.

The Henchman appeared between the two. "Brad," he offered, "I have an idea. We may be able to drive this thing through these doors after all."

That seemed to sate the mascot, at least temporarily.

"Gather 'round. We're gonna need everybody," Dutch instructed.

The plan was simple. Even though there were no drivable cars in front of the arena, there were still openings in the wreckage wide enough for the Cattle-ac to fit. The arena proper sat in the center of the bowl shape formed by the Cow Palace grounds, so the aisles of cars sloped up and away from the building. And, as luck would have it, there was a row that led from the top of the lot directly down into the ticket window courtyard and up to the main entry doors. They could drive the Tauros up, away from the entry, along the aisle, one hundred yards out and at a total incline of twenty feet or so. Once there, all they'd need to do was turn the vehicle around and put it in neutral, and with five of them pushing, the idea was they would get the car going fast enough to smash through the doors – or at least damage them enough so they could get in.

Once The Henchman explained the idea to the group and there were several heads nodding in agreement, everyone looked at Brad. His anger had subsided and so now he simply looked surly.

"Well," he asked, "can I still drive?"

They all replied in unison, "Yes!"

Only then did he break into a wide grin.

Everyone had a good laugh for a bit before Brad offered, "I'm sorry I snapped. I got locked out of an arena during the World Leapfrog Championships a few years ago and I guess I never got over it. Plus, I really need to get paid for this gig."

The bullfighter nodded in agreement before changing the subject. "We hurry. It dark soon."

The man was right, and by the time the Cattle-ac made the slow trek up the aisle and completed the nine-point turn in order to change directions, it was pitch black. The rain that had subsided for about an hour began again, just a sprinkle at first. The only light to see by was coming from the vehicle itself. Power was apparently out all over the region.

Brad settled in behind the steering wheel and, for safety, put his cow head on, carefully positioning it so he could almost see straight down the ramp toward the arena entryway. The remaining members of the group positioned themselves behind the back bumper of the massive Tauros and began to shove. It took quite an effort just to get the car to move, but once it did, the Cattle-ac descended the slope in a hurry.

Right off the bat the huge vehicle began to veer to the right and looked as though it would soon crash into a pile of coupes.

The Henchman called out from behind the car, "Brad, steer!"

The mascot had taken his hooves off the steering wheel and had lifted them high into the air, ready to let out a full-fledged and vigorous, "Whee!" as if he was on a roller coaster.

It was tough for him to turn his head to see and so, still looking forward, he called out, "What?"

"I said 'steer!'" yelled The Henchman. A rather confusing interaction began.

"What?"

"Steer, Brad, steer!"

"No, cow!"

"What?"

"I said, 'cow!'"

"No, I mean steer!"

"No, I am a cow!"

"No, Brad, steer. Steer the car! You're gonna crash!"

"Oh!" Brad exclaimed, giving a hard tug on the Cattle-ac's steering wheel.

The vehicle straightened out, narrowly avoiding clipping the coupe pile. Gravity and inertia set in and, aided by the initial thrust of the launching team and Brad's expert steering, the car was soon out of reach of the five-member pit crew. Down the sloped aisle the Cattle-ac sped, gaining speed as it dropped, before leveling out in the flat courtyard in front of the entry doors. Brad once again lifted his hooves high in the air and let out not the expected roller coaster "Whee!" but a rather exuberant and animated "Moo!"

With the five others sprinting down the aisle behind him, yelling their support, Brad the mascot guided the oversized Tauros directly into the center of the bank of arena doors.

Just before impact, Red Simford came around the corner of the massive structure, from the direction of the truck section and the RV where the group had enjoyed friendly banter and hot tea a short while earlier.

Flashlight in hand, Red let out a loud, "What in tarnation?" right before his prized Cattle-ac, driven, it appeared, by a cow, and followed by a leaping cheering section, rammed headlong into the middle of the arena entry doors.

The front of the vehicle and several of the doors crumbled in a foot or two with a tremendous crashing sound, and Brad's cow head went flying forward, again bouncing away off one of the doors. Both Red and the push party arrived at the Tauros at about the same time, just as Brad was climbing out of the car. They all stared at one another for a bit, except for Dutch, who didn't want to make eye contact with anyone. His eyes were darting about in search of something to focus on. Red was mad, so much so that his face matched his name, and The Henchman knew he was about to bear the brunt of the oversized man's wrath.

Plus, the doors to the arena were still closed and locked tight, though a few of them had good-sized dents in them. They were closed, that is, until a door at the right end of the run opened up, and a head popped out.

It was Pajuna, the leader of the Horro bike gang.

He glanced at the wreckage in front of him, the stunned men standing around what, in the dark, seemed to be piles of twisted metal out in what had been the sales lot. Surprise mixed with confusion and sleep on the biker's countenance.

Pajuna rubbed his eyes and yawned, and then asked, "What happened here?"

"Devon, would you consider yourself a good swimmer?" Dr. Herens asked the college student.

The torrent of water continued to rush into the basement and was rising over the height of the desks on which the two had sought refuge. They once again found themselves standing in water.

The young man considered the question a bit and answered, "I can dog paddle if I need to, we just need to figure out how we're going to get out of here. Why do you ask, Professor?"

"Well, Devon, I'm thinking we're going to have to swim our way out of here, maybe over to the elevator shaft and then somehow float our way up. The current is quite strong, but we do have that board." Devon was holding on to the brightly colored boogie board. It had drawings of cows and seabirds all over it.

Herens continued, "Plus, I'm more than a little concerned that the piranha tank got knocked over. I mean, they don't usually attack healthy creatures, but these guys have been subjected to genetic science of some sort."

Devon stared for a moment at the professor after this latest statement, digesting the information – hopefully before a school of carnivorous fish digested him. He scrambled a few feet up to the top of the cubicle partition, balancing himself over it like he was straddling a fence.

"Okay, now I *am* freaked out about all of this water in here!"

He rapidly scanned the rising water. In the poor light, the water looked dark green, and with all of the papers and cubicle contents floating around, it was impossible to see if any man-eating fish were in the vicinity. Devon was starting to panic.

"How can those fish be alive in salt water anyway?" he asked.

"Well, a lot of the Amazon, down near the delta where it enters the ocean, is salty I'd assume," the professor replied. "Plus, with the typhoon, there's bound to be a lot of rain-water in here. This isn't all from the ocean surge, Devon."

"That didn't help the situation," Devon thought. "Don't you think you should climb up out of there?" he asked.

Herens was now standing in about a foot of water, even though he was up on a desktop.

"Perhaps you're right, Devon."

The professor climbed atop the cubicle wall, being careful not to disturb one of the few remaining light sticks. *"It's time to act,"* he thought.

Devon was on the verge of losing it. The young scientist kept scanning the water, searching for piranha. The boogie board had a small rope attached to its front end, and Devon had it wrapped around his right wrist and was holding it tightly.

"Okay, that's it!" the teacher said confidently. "This is what we're going to do. You are going to lie on top of that boogie board and point it toward the elevator shaft. Your job is to kick your feet like crazy. As hard as you can. Got it?"

Devon nodded.

Herens had the young man's attention, so before fear could paralyze him, the professor continued. "I will hop in next to you, grab ahold of the back of your board and push. I was a pretty good swimmer in my day."

"You were?" Devon asked.

"Most certainly. I was on the AAU team that finished fifth in the Swim and Sandwich Games back in the eighties. I can do the Blue Lingo stroke like nobody's business."

Devon had never heard of either the games or the stroke. All he wanted was to get out, but he was really concerned about the piranhas.

"What about the fish, Dr. Herens?" he asked.

"Oh fish, smish. That knife display case we saw earlier may still be there, and it is directly in the path of the shaft. If I need to, I'll grab one of those bad boys out of the case. If the piranha bother us, we'll be eating fish for dinner, my son!"

The professor's confidence inspired Devon, which is exactly what the teacher wanted. The fact of the matter was he had no clue what the meat-eating swimmers would do. He thought fish wouldn't bother them, but it was more of an educated guess than anything. Of course, he wasn't about to tell Devon that.

The student eased himself down into the cold water and onto the boogie board, and aligned himself with where he thought the open elevator was. Within seconds, the professor was right next to him, realizing that, since the water was still only chest high, he could actually walk and push the Devon-laden boogie board forward. The floor was quite slippery and, truth be told, once they made it into the meat of the current, he didn't know if walking or swimming would be the better option. But for now, walking was best.

The professor grabbed a couple of light sticks off the top of a nearby cubicle and handed them to Devon. The duo took off. Despite the teacher slipping a time or two, the pair reached the knife display cabinet, some fifteen feet away, quickly. The case was bobbing up and down, pinned against a still-standing cubicle wall, held in place by what so far was a fairly mild current. They each grabbed a weapon. The professor held his in the hand that was not guiding the boogie board, and Devon, his hands occupied with light sticks, placed the blade of his between his teeth.

They were nearly halfway to their goal and, though they could not yet see the elevator shaft, the current they were heading into was getting stronger. The rushing water was louder here too, and its level had risen to just under the professor's armpits.

"You ready, Devon?" Dr. Herens asked.

The student nodded. The professor began again to push in earnest. Devon kicked his feet rapidly, splashing water everywhere.

Almost immediately, the young man spit out the knife blade and screamed, "Wait! Stop!" and added, "What the hell is that?"

At the periphery of their vision, at the edge of the circle of light created by Devon's light sticks, something was headed directly for the pair.

The professor couldn't see it at first and asked, "Is it the fish, Devon?"

This was no school of piranha, and the boogie board occupant shouted, "You gotta be kidding me! It's a snake! It's like a giant boa constrictor or something."

Without hesitation, Professor Herens began to pull, rather than push, on the board. Too panicked to simply turn around and head the other way, they floundered their way toward the back of the room. The professor turned and faced the back wall. Devon tried to help but in his agitation managed only to splash his light sticks in the water in front of the boogie board. Herens' feet kept slipping and he dropped completely underwater a few times, but in the end they outpaced the danger and made it back to relative, albeit temporary, safety at the top of the cubicle partitions in the back of the basement. The water was now just a couple of inches from the tops of the cubicles.

As they both caught their breath, again they glimpsed the slithering being. It was making its way directly toward the back wall. Directly toward them. The professor held his knife forward in a defensive position, the small blade now seeming quite inadequate against the oncoming threat. He glanced over at Devon, who was looking across the water in sudden realization that he'd dropped his weapon.

But once the serpentine figure got closer, close enough for its details to be made out in the dim green light, Professor

Herens let out a hearty laugh. Devon glanced over at the man, thinking he'd lost his mind.

The professor saw Devon's expression and made a patting motion with his hands. "Devon, it's not a snake."

"It's not?" he asked incredulously. Devon took a hard look. It still looked like a snake to him. A really large snake.

The thing was now in arm's reach. To Devon's amazement, the professor reached down and grabbed it.

He repeated, "Devon, it's not a snake." He added, "It's a fire hose." Herens smiled. "Someone's trying to rescue us."

And then a loud voice was heard, a voice Devon recognized. It resonated down through the elevator shaft and out across the top of the water, now nearly six feet deep in the basement of the Floral and Dance Sciences building at AAU. As if amplified by a bullhorn or some other device, the voice of deliverance rang out.

"Señor Devon. If you are down there, grab the hose. I pull you out. Señor Devon, grab the hose."

It was Caceres, come to save the day.

I CAN TAKE NO MORE. THIS HUMAN WOMAN IS DRESSED IN THE SKINS OF MY SPECIES. SHE MUST PAY. THEY ALL MUST PAY. FOR TOO LONG COWS HAVE BEEN ABUSED BY THE HUMANS. FOR TOO LONG HAVE WE GIVEN OUR MILK, OUR LIVES AND NOW IT APPEARS OUR SKINS AS WELL. FOR THE SAKE OF ALL COWDOM I WILL EXECUTE JUSTICE. THE BEEF I HAVE WITH THE HUMANS IS LEGITIMATE. IT IS TIME FOR REVENGE. I SHALL DIRECT THE OTHERS.

"Moooooaarrrgghhheeeeeeee!"

AH, LOOK HOW THE HUMANS COWER. LOOK HOW THE WINDOWS SHATTER. THE OTHERS ARE IN AGREEMENT. IT IS TIME TO MOVE FORWARD. IT IS TIME TO BE HEARD.

There was no reason for either Officer Holstein or Ivory Chateaubriand to have guessed that the bull-like creature before them was engaged in a constant internal monologue. At the time, the pair was just trying to absorb it all, trying to fathom the sudden and strange sight.

Like some warped and insane Wild West showdown from another dimension, the two officers stood facing a row of creatures that appeared intent on their destruction. In the middle of the line of horror stood the beast that seemed to be the leader, an enormous horned monster of somewhat bovine beginnings. The creature was staring at Ivory and lost in thought at the same time, wearing a threatening look of impending doom.

And if the leader was enormous, the being to its left was ridiculously large. It looked like an ordinary dairy cow, but was the size of a large elephant. It too seemed to be staring right through Assistant Deputy Chateaubriand. On the other side of the apparent captain of the chaos was a creature half cow, half dragon. With a ridge of spiked plates along its back and some sort of bizarre, metallic tail, the beast had smoke streaming out of both nostrils. The darn thing looked like it could potentially breathe fire.

To the right of this brute stood another monstrosity, a cow-like quadruped that seemed to have giant bags on each of its sides. A green, ominous liquid oozed from the gland-like openings on each of the totes. Both the be-satcheled creature and the dragon-cow also glared menacingly at Ivory. In fact, they all did, save for the three small ones who had broken rank and who were rummaging around the gutters along Lineback Street, which were jammed up with all sorts of debris. Every few seconds, one of the little trio would locate something it deemed edible and would tear into it, shark-like teeth ravenously ripping the find apart. Instantly, its two companions would be right there, apparently drawn by the sounds of shredding. In a flash, the snack would be nonexistent and off the three would scurry, noses in the water in search of additional prey. They were continually running into each other and obstacles in their path.

"Officer Holstein, perhaps we should get back into the leather store," Ivory whispered.

"I think that would perhaps be a really bad idea," the policeman answered, also in a quiet tone. "I think these things have a problem with leather." The detective side of the policeman had deduced that the ominous glaring from these creatures in the direction of his assistant deputy was due to her new attire.

"Okay, well what do you suggest?" Ivory asked.

Holstein was mulling over that very thought when the center beast, the one with the horns, lowered his head and began to moo.

At first the call was low-pitched, barely audible but still able to shake the ground, like the impact from the stereo system of a suspension-lowered automobile with its bass turned up high. Gradually the moo rose in tone to that of a common cow moo, but one amplified to the decibel level of a small jet engine. And as the pitch went up, it got louder, the reverberation so severe that both the officer and the assistant deputy had to cover their ears for protection. Higher and louder the monster's voice rose, until it morphed into a sort of combination roar, wail and scream. At its apex, when it seemed the moo could not possibly continue, a shock wave blew out from the throat of the mutated bull. It knocked both Chris and Ivory backwards and right off their feet. They were both rendered unconscious when they slammed down onto the sidewalk. And, at the same time, all of the front display windows shattered to pieces in each of the businesses down Lineback Street, right up to, but not including the Chicken Coop restaurant.

Once the wave subsided, the creatures, including the little ones who were now back in line, began to march toward the prostrate duo. Several rapid-fire lightning strikes lit up the darkening sky, with thunder so intense the ground shook yet again. Beefy looked up into newly intensified rain, purple eyes squinting through the downpour. A renewed wind roared down Lineback, staggering the mutated cattle. They dug their respective hooves into the concrete of the boulevard. Beefy seemed to smile.

NOW, MY HERD. WITH ME. IT IS TIME TO FINISH THIS.

Aliab Dinka lived to surf.

A lifetime resident of Bay City, the twenty-year-old couldn't remember a day when he wasn't out riding the waves. Lately accompanied by a novice surfing enthusiast, a recent transplant to the West Coast named Dingo Nellie, Aliab felt most at home in the ocean. The part-time lifeguard and sometime college student lived in a tiny house in the Berrenda Bluff neighborhood of Bay City. It seemed the entire Bay City surfing community resided within the three blocks known as the Bluffs. They formed a sort of barrier between the Mashona neighborhood and the tall cliffs that rose out of the Pacific.

Aliab continually monitored the ocean and was acutely and intensely aware of even subtle changes in the surf. At any given time, he could describe the height, pace and direction of the waves that were breaking just down the long staircase that had been built into the cliffside. On two separate occasions the young man had sounded the alarm, heard both throughout the Bluffs and around the world via technology, that the Marinhoa, the mother of all impromptu come-as-you-are-but-get-here-fast international surf competitions, was set to begin, right there and right then. Surfers across the globe await the call heralding the start of the Marinhoa surf extravaganza, and converge on that setting in a sort of crazy, international surfer migration. The Marinhoa is called during only the most intense of surfing conditions at whatever location those conditions exist. Continual, forty- to fifty-foot waves over a three- to four-day period are the norm for the Marinhoa, and, because the time and location of such events are random and impossible to predict, diehard surfers around the world are always at the ready, set to grab a board and hop a plane in order to get to the location of the Marinhoa in time to participate in the competition. Aliab was no exception, and wore his wetsuit at all times, even when attending random classes at AAU, just in case he got the call a Marinhoa was in the works.

The sudden and dramatic increase in the wave size and frequency on this day had surprised the ocean veteran. It was as if out of nowhere huge waves had formed and were breaking nearly against the cliff wall down at the beach below Aliab's residence. He'd already been out a couple of times earlier, and the ocean had been so calm he'd done more paddling than catching waves of any substance. Still, a day on the water was better than a day not on the water, as Aliab would often say.

Once the sun set, however, it seemed as if the ocean had come alive. Aliab could hear the difference in the waves. These breakers were slamming home, which was a surprising and welcome turn of events for the surfer, who was not unaccustomed to night surfing. It was a common activity for folks from the Bluffs.

Aliab and Dingo were sharing a snack of fruit from a can when Aliab's keen hearing caught the sudden change from down in the surf.

"Dude, do you hear that?" Aliab was up and headed to the kitchen window.

It was pitch black outside, and it had begun to rain. He wasn't looking for anything, but the young man slid open the window so he could get a better listen.

"I don't hear anything, dude," Dingo answered.

Aliab knew in a flash what to do. He instructed his friend, "Find your phone and call Piney Woods. Tell him we've got a Marinhoa event. Then grab your longboard and get down to the water. It's a radical wave-train."

And without waiting for a response, Aliab grabbed his tri-fin and sprinted out the door. He rang the large cowbell, which hung on a rope from a rafter on the front porch, several times and was gone. Dingo began searching for her phone, hidden somewhere, she knew, under either a four-foot pile of clothes or a six-foot stack of pizza boxes.

"A radical wave-train?" she said to herself as she searched. "Righteous, dude."

When she thought about it, Margaret O'Leary figured there were a whole lot of things that could be on fire, caused by a whole lot of other things in and around Contented Corners. As she made her way through the front gate and up the soggy drive toward the farm structures, lightning continued to regularly flash on the horizon in all directions. The flames ahead shot some fifty feet into the sky. But the trees that lined the driveway blocked visual confirmation of the more important details of the blaze, owing to the easy curves in the roadway leading back into the farm. Margaret was left to speculate on the nature of the inferno.

An old woman who'd just been in a horrendous and traumatizing accident, Margaret wasn't moving at top speed as she passed the mailbox, a few feet onto the property from Highway One. Even in the best of shape, she would be given a run for her money in a sprint with a blue-grey tortoise, and a tired one at that. The more than leisurely pace gave Margaret plenty of time to consider the possible origins of the fire ahead. A bolt from the god of thunder, that sexy guy with the hammer, was the most likely source of the inferno that was still not yet in view, she figured.

Mrs. O'Leary expected the farmhouse or oak tree to be on fire, or perhaps even the barn itself. She seemed to remember thinking about the fact that the coffee pot and electric carpet sweeper robot were both turned on when she and John had bolted out of there. Perhaps the same flood that had toppled the semitruck had knocked the coffee pot onto the robot and it had wandered throughout the grounds spilling coffee everywhere. That might start a fire, she reasoned.

Margaret shuffled along another ten feet. She thought about the old black and white movie John had been watching, *Hidee*. She always loved that film, particularly the part where the little girl sneaks her pet cow into a dormitory to get it out of a driving rainstorm.

"This day has become life imitating art," she thought, chuckling as she remembered the scene from the movie where Hidee tries to hide her cow in a child-sized bed.

It was John's television that had launched her down this line of thought. Perhaps the door to the farmhouse had blown open in the storm and the wind had knocked over the television and the farmhouse was on fire.

She hobbled around a gentle turn in the driveway toward the back of the farm. It was then that a quick thought, a sudden memory, jogged her awareness, and Mrs. O'Leary became convinced that she knew what was on fire and what had most likely caused it.

To aid in the process of escorting the cows out of the barn and onto the truck, Margaret had fired up an old lantern that

John kept on a hook just inside the main doors, right next to a shelf holding a box of stick matches. She didn't remember turning the lantern off before she and John had gone rumbling away from the farm. Now certain the barn was on fire and she, or an unnoticed kick from one of the cows, had started it, the woman let out a barely audible "Oh my!" and sped up. Though uncertain what she would do once she got there, Mrs. O'Leary, now hustling, covered the next twelve feet in just under five minutes.

Once everything was explained, the situation at the Cow Palace almost seemed somewhat amusing to one and all, even the typically gruff Red Simford. Yes, despite the fact he'd just lost quite a bit of new car inventory, and the grill of his custom Cattle-ac had been severely damaged, the over-sized Tauros dealer did manage to offer up the slightest of smiles, but only after the whole situation had been sorted out. Once Red smiled, everyone felt a little bit better about smashing up his car. Except Pajuna, who was still in a daze about the whole thing.

During the time of the intense hailstorm that was devastating the portion of the Cow Palace parking lot occupied by the huge RV and the assorted trucks, an even deadlier episode had occurred just around the corner of the lot, at the front entry to both the car sale and the Cow Palace itself: a tornado had touched down.

Once the funnel cloud hit the ground at the back end of the lot, two beautiful, new Tauros three-wheeled mini-convertible coupes had been lifted up into the air a hundred feet, only to be unceremoniously dropped two rows away on top of several pink and aqua Tauros mail carrier models.

After that, as the tornado had wandered aimlessly throughout the lot, cars had been tossed about like so many of those little sticks in that game played with little sticks. And, as if outrunning a runaway tornado, Horro gang bikers and Brain Trusters had torn out of there, everyone leaping onto whatever motorcycle was nearest. More than a half a dozen bikes could be seen racing toward the main entrance with a gang member on the front and a Brain Truster on the back. In a couple of instances, it was the Brain Truster that took the handlebars, with a startled Horro just hanging on for dear life.

Red had tried to calm everyone down, shouting out "Consarn it!" and "Doshblast ya!" at every opportunity in a futile attempt to slow the mass exodus. Within just a few minutes, however, everyone had taken off and Red was standing guard in front of his prized Cattle-ac, willing to do whatever it took to protect the three-rowed super-car. He wouldn't share what his plan of attack was in case he had to square off with the twister; the big man just shared that he wasn't about to let the darn beast of a storm harm "Ol' Longhorn," as he sometimes liked to call the vehicle. Driving away from the menacing tornado had been out of the question due to the low top speed of the Cattle-ac, so if push had come to shove, Red just would most likely have wrassled the twister over the fate of his beloved car.

Luckily, things never got that far as the sudden tornado vaporized into nothing as quickly as it had formed, a mere ten yards from Red and the Cattle-ac. Once he'd re-gathered his wits and ensured his loins were girded, he set off to inspect the damage to the car inventory as well as check to see if anyone needed any assistance. Before heading off in a clockwise direction around the perimeter of the arena, the big man had locked the front entry doors up tight to make sure no varmints or rustlers got to all the valuable financial information inside the place, seeing as how all the knuckle-headed Brain Trusters who had been stationed at the picnic tables in there had evacuated with the biker gang.

Red had just turned the corner when Dutch and the RV refugees had come around the other side. While The Henchman and his charges were trying to figure out how to break down the front doors to the Cow Palace arena, Red was lamenting the fact that the car inventory was a total loss and, of course, looking for injured folks. Gone were the sports saloons, family sedans and executive mid-luxury touring cars. Gone were the pony cars, hot hatches and muscle minivans. The entire lineup of vehicles, previously in pristine condition, had been completely destroyed by either hailstorm, tornado or a wicked combination of the two.

Dutch Friesian then explained how the sextet had avoided certain death from grapefruit-sized ice balls, and their furious attempt the get inside the arena to rescue Red and anyone who had happened to escape the carnage. The Henchman admitted to being completely baffled by the possible cause of the extra-horrific destruction they stumbled upon when he turned the corner; heck they all were.

"I wasn't sure what happened, boss. I just figured you were in trouble and whatever had thrown those cars around had you locked inside the building with it."

Each of the other members of the little RV survivors club nodded. They too thought something sinister had happened.

Red now let himself laugh heartily, a huge oversized belly laugh reminiscent, The Henchman thought, of the one he had laughed when Dutch was explaining the entertainment lineup for the car sale.

"That seems like a hundred miles ago," Dutch thought.

Simford gave The Henchman an oversized and rather uncomfortable hug and said, "Aww heck, ya weasel. What'd ya think happened, the Monster Cow of the Cow Palace got me?"

He broke again into a gigantic howl and this time, everyone joined in, though they really didn't know why.

The Spanish European laughed most of all, at first putting both of his hands down on his knees, half bowled over in hilarity, and then leaning far back and offering up loud guffaws to the stormy skies. Salers Salorn continued his gay howl and started swishing his cape about and sashaying out into the darkness among the piles of automobiles. He didn't notice that everyone, including Red, who usually out-laughed everyone, had stopped and was staring at him. Had he noticed, he probably wouldn't have cared anyway, so lost was he in his world of laughing and swishing.

Red offered up a "What in tarnation?" Pajuna looked even more confused than before.

Dutch simply said, "The man has been under a lot of stress."

The rest of the assembly managed to combine nodding in agreement with a side-to-side, disapproving shake of the head. It was quite unusual to see the five of them – Red, Han, Shorty, Brad and Siri – all try to nod up and down and side to side at the same time.

Noticing this display, Pajuna simply shut the door and disappeared back into the dark arena.

The tale of Red's circumnavigation of the Cow Palace continued. He had arrived at the truck section of the lot and had seen the impact damage to all of the rigs in the area, and then noticed the RV parked toward the back fence. He'd forgotten about the DBP and had hustled back to see if perhaps anyone was stuck inside. He'd found nobody home, but the television was turned on to a charming old movie and there was a half a pot of tea on the range, so he settled in to warm up a bit.

"I drank some tea, must've dozed off," Red admitted.

In a move that surprised them all, Dutch turned and looked up, glaring at his boss. "You did what?" He asked.

The little man was suddenly quite agitated, a side of himself he'd never shown to Red before. The car dealer could tell there was something wrong. Heck, everyone could tell. Dutch clenched his fists, and his face started to swell up and flush. This sure came out of nowhere.

"Now, calm yourself down. I'm sorry I called ya a weasel again. Yer my The Henchman and always will be. I was just funnin'. And I forgive you for smashing up Ol' Longhorn. We'll get him fixed. I mean, why cry over spilt milk?"

The Henchman erupted. "Good *God*! You just don't get it! Nobody gets it!"

Just then, Salers Salorn came swishing in from the darkness, waving his cape in full circular motion, though his laughter was now down to a quiet chuckle. Just as quickly, he was gone again, swishing his way back to the truck side of the arena.

Red returned to the subject at hand: the irate employee. "Why don't you just settle on down and tell me what the problem is. Is it because I think I may have fallen asleep watching that incredibly entertaining movie?"

Now totally defeated, Dutch quit screaming and let out a long sigh. "It's a tragic error, that's all."

"For corn's sake! What is? What are you talkin' about?" Red clenched his fists. He was starting to lose his cool.

Brad, who always knew how to break up a tense moment, had taken the opportunity, while everyone was distracted by the bullfighter's swishing, to re-don his brown cow head.

He now stepped up between Red and Dutch. "Pardon my *mooooving* in here. I was just *milking* it back there. *Butter* tell us what's up, Mr. Frownyface. Say *cheese!*"

He held his hoof-hand up in front of his face like he was holding a camera, making a pressing motion as though he was taking a photo. This routine had never failed him but, in this situation, it didn't seem to quite have the impact he was hoping for.

Red pushed the cow mascot out of the way and stooped down so he was face to face with The Henchman.

He stared at the little man's darting eyes until eye contact was established. "Out with it. What's got you so riled?"

"Nobody, and I mean nobody, gives a wild steer's patooey about the fact that I am passionate about tea. I've dedicated my life to tea. I've gone to school to learn about tea. I read books, go to seminars, make my own blends, everything. I am a tea master! Nobody cares." Dutch looked down at his shoes.

"Why do you think I have you make tea for our best customers? I care, and I like your tea. I probably fell asleep because the tea was so good."

"You don't even know what you did wrong, that's the sad part." Dutch muttered.

"Yer losin' me, kid," Red replied. He turned to the group. "Anybody else gettin' this stuff?"

Nobody appeared to be.

The Henchman raised his head and addressed the group. "I don't expect any of you to get this, but it is simply not done. You never, never, never over-steep a pot of tea. It's not done. You don't cook it too long, it ruins the flavor, it destroys the blend." He looked back at Red. "It's like you were drinking the equivalent of the sole of a leather shoe. I don't even know why I'm mad at you. It's my tea, it's my blend. I left the pot on, and I feel horrible that anyone was subject to such a... such a... such an abomination. And you actually drank it. I just don't believe it."

Dutch was completely despondent, more exhausted now than upset. He let out a sort of whimpering sound.

Everyone then spoke at once, kindly encouraging The Henchman with compliments about his fantastic tea and, to a greater degree, his fantastic tea-making ability. Siri

Batangas, utilizing perfect timing to go with his perfect old-time movie actor impersonation, capped the round of uplifting talk with an "I say, old chap. If anyone knows tea, I know tea. And by golly, yours is the finest tea in the entirety of her majesty's wide and wonderful kingdom."

That seemed to bring Dutch out of his funk. It had been a stressful day for everyone, including the bullfighter, whom they found absorbed in an encore presentation of *Hidee*, which was playing on the widescreen television when they all made it back to the DBP. The group insisted Dutch brew up a fresh batch for one and all, and Red declared they should spend the rest of the night in the relative safety of the giant home on wheels, particularly since it appeared the power was out in the arena. They all figured that Pajuna would be safe inside the Cow Palace, however. The biker gang leader was clearly unfazed by the darkness inside and probably could take care of himself better than most.

So, into the RV the seven settled for what they hoped would be an uneventful night. Help could be secured come daybreak, they reasoned. And, as the rain began once more to intensify, the teakettle started to toot and the movie really got to the good part, the Cow Palace crew felt confident things would get much better once the sun rose.

They had no idea how horribly wrong they were.

🐂🐂🐂

The boogie board made towing at first Devon and then Dr. Herens through the strong current much easier. During their respective turns, each man laid flat across the board, holding tightly on to the fire hose and kicking his feet for propulsion. And once in the shaft itself, the hose was cinched around the waist of the rescuee and he walked, repelled, and was lifted up the side of the shaft, directly through the waterfall.

The elevator itself was stuck at the third floor, and Caceres, with the fire hose, a powerful flashlight and a bullhorn at his disposal, was on the second floor. The water was rushing into the shaft from the first-floor main lobby, and, as Devon and the professor were hoisted past, they each thought they could make out a lake a couple of feet deep covering the lobby floor.

Nobody was sure why the lobby door to the elevator shaft was open, but it was most likely the result of some power grid malfunction. On the upper floors, some but not all of the lights were on, the reason for which was another mystery for everyone.

Hoisting Devon up from the first to second floor took no small effort, but Caceres managed it. Once Devon was rescued, pulling the professor out of the nearly filled basement went much faster, as Caceres and Devon were both able to pull on the fire hose. The only incident came when the professor broke into a panic, calling out for the duo to pull and pull fast. When Dr. Herens was about ten feet from the elevator shaft, laid out on the boogie board, the water had erupted into a roiling circle of activity just a few feet away. The bubbling and intense splashing was, of course, the school of piranha, devouring a delicious something or other. The professor was convinced he was about to be dessert. But, within a few seconds, the intense activity subsided and several dozen pieces of plastic had come to the surface, a couple in arm's reach of the teacher. He had carefully grabbed ahold of one of them and held it close to his eyes, breaking into laughter once he was able to decipher through the darkness the bits of writing on the remnant. It was a piece of wrapping from a two-pound bag of carrots. Those darned students had done it – they'd created vegan piranha.

Before too long, the trio was standing in Dr. Herens' office. Fortunately, this was one of the spaces where the lighting still worked. As Devon and the professor dried off with some paper towels, Caceres told them about how he happened to be there, as it turned out, just in the nick of time.

The most confusing part of Caceres' explanation had to do with the fact that he thought a gigantic python was headed toward Contented Corners and that was the reason for the sudden evacuation. It was the professor who finally figured out that somehow the word "typhoon" had been lost in translation and had become the word "python."

They all laughed, with Herens chiming in, "I suppose it would have to be some sort of a mutated gigantic python to be of such a threat. Now that sounds like the plot of a bad movie."

They all chuckled some more.

There were a few other bits of the saga of Caceres that had to be translated to be understood, but in the end, Devon and the professor figured they had the overall gist of what had gone down.

Once the rain had begun, John, Mrs. O'Leary and Caceres all understood from Devon's phone call that they had to get out, be the reason a snake or a storm (or a rich businessman). Once the cows were loaded into the flatbed, Mr. Steerman had asked Caceres to head over to the university to make sure Devon was okay. He'd handed him written directions to find both the School of Floral and Dance Sciences building and Devon's cubicle. He also wrote down Devon's phone number and the name of his teacher, Dr. Herens.

The School of Floral and Dance Sciences building was built into the side of a large hill and there were two primary entrances. Most folks came in on the first floor, which opened into a large quad area. The campus bookstore, several kiosk businesses, the popular American Grill, the library and the School of Equestrian Psychology building were also adjacent to the quad. It was the primary gathering place for students, right off the main road leading down to the campus from Highway One. People loved to congregate and visit, eat or study under a tree, on a concrete bench or just stretched out on the lawn, right at sea level and just a few hundred yards from the serene waves of the Pacific.

This entire area had been hit hard by the storm surge. The university's old Bianca Val Padana water tower, named after one of the school's first benefactors, had toppled and its thirty thousand gallons of water were launched directly into the front of the very building that Devon and Dr. Herens occupied.

Unable to access the building from the lower level, Caceres had taken a secondary, upper road, Stripsteak Street, behind the building. He accessed the building through the sixth-floor entrance at the back. The funny thing was, John had told Caceres he might have to get in that way. Everyone wondered how the man could have known.

The power was out intermittently on the floor, so Caceres had gone back to the pickup and grabbed the flashlight from the glove box. The elevators were also out and so he'd made his way as far as possible down the stairwell. His intent was to take the stairs all the way down to the basement, but he was stopped at the first floor by the flood that was crashing onto the stairs from the main lobby.

Backtracking, the rescuer headed back up to the sixth floor where an informational display kiosk listed the room numbers for all of the professors. He found the room number belonging to Dr. Herring and turned back around, descending the stairs once again to get to the correct floor. He managed to find Dr. Herring's office, but found nothing in there that could be of use in a rescue attempt.

But as luck would have it, Dr. Herring, a tenured professor in the Gerber Daisy Studies Department, had his office right next to Dr. Herens'. Once Caceres was inside the correct office, he had found the bullhorn and his rescue plan came into focus. All he needed was a fire hose and that was simple enough to find. The School of Hose Anatomy occupied about half of the fourth floor and there were dozens of them there.

By the time Caceres finished relaying the details of his rescue efforts, his two benefactors had partially, if not sufficiently, dried off, so they all headed back up the stairs toward the pickup. Neither Devon nor the professor owned an automobile, and both reasoned it would be a waste of time to try to find their respective bicycles out in the flood, though Devon did boast that, if he only had his ten-speed, he'd probably make better time in the killer typhoon than any car would.

The idea was to head back to Contented Corners. The kind teacher offered to come along and lend whatever assistance he could. Caceres could not confirm that Devon's dad and Mrs. O'Leary had made it out before the ocean surge came inland. It was dark and raining moderately once they exited the building and visibility was quite limited. This was most likely a good thing, because if Devon had seen the destruction splayed out below him in the quad, he would have been even more worried about his dad, Mrs. O'Leary and Contented Corners. Oh, for certain he was worried as it was, he just would have been even more worried had he seen the devastation.

The professor slid in through the passenger door, Devon right behind him. Caceres opened the driver side door, but, before he climbed in, movement in the bed of the truck caught his attention. It was the aardvarks Mrs. O'Leary had loaded in. In the rush to get away from the farm, Caceres hadn't noticed them.

"Ah, my friends," Caceres said. "How you get here? You swim?" The aardvarks didn't answer.

KENANA, TOSS THE MALE ON YOUR BACK. ACTIVATE YOUR ADHESION FIELD. I SHALL TAKE THE WOMAN DRESSED IN THE SKINS OF OUR ANCESTORS. WE SHALL HERD THESE TWO EVIL HUMANS A SHORT WAY WEST FROM HERE, WHERE MY SENSES TELL ME THERE IS A LARGE CLIFF OFF WHICH WE MAY SUMMARILY LAUNCH THEM, LAUNCH THEM TO THEIR DEATHS. MOO, MOO, MOO. WE SHALL BURN THEM IN ACID, BURN THEM IN FIRE AND THROW THEM TO THE MURKY DEPTHS BELOW. AND ONCE THEY ARE DECEASED, YOU SHALL FEED, LITTLE ONES. FEED YOU SHALL, ON THE CARCASSES OF THE DEFILERS. MOO, MOO, MOO.

Once Officer Holstein regained consciousness, it took him a while to get his bearings. He was flat on his back. He could sense motion, as if being carried along. He felt a gentle jostling up and down. He guessed he was on the back of some giant animal. The rain was falling again, quite heavily, but the wind had died down. And it was dark.

He tried to sit up, but was held flat in place by some force he could not identify. The officer could move his arms, which were flat on his chest, and conducted a brief self-pat down to make sure his parts were intact. They were, and the officer's stun gun was resting in his hip-strapped holster.

Holstein turned his head to the right and saw two rows of rooftops leading away from him. He looked the other direction and noticed he was about fifty feet in front of some sort of concrete tower. Canchim Tower!

A sudden memory rushed back into his head, forcing out the grogginess. It was the cows, those mutated-beyond-belief creatures with the purple eyes. The bull with the giant horns. He and his assistant deputy had been face to face with the bovine row of terror. And then there was the moo. That demented and horrific moo. The policeman remembered being thrown back, and then nothing.

"*Oh no,*" he thought suddenly. "*I've got to get to Ivory.*"

He struggled in earnest to prop himself up, but again couldn't budge. Something was holding him firm.

Holstein blinked his eyes against the rain and tried hard to listen for any clue that might give him more information about what was happening, and, more importantly, about the status of Mrs. Chateaubriand. But listen as he might, all he could hear was the recording his brain was playing over and over, like a skip on the world's most terrifying record.

The moo. The moo from hell.

ᏫᎦ ᏫᎦ ᏫᎦ

John Steerman took a long look at what had been his delightful little herd of cows. The pastoral pleasantness of Contented Corners seemed an eternity away. Was it just yesterday that he and Lactose Tolerant were playing hopscotch bingo out behind the barn?

The creatures in front of him bore no resemblance to the herd he'd hand-raised. These were more like purple-eyed, mostly uddered freaks of nature, hell-bent on some as yet unknown death and destruction. After he'd received his sprinting orders from Mrs. O'Leary, the farmer had hustled up Highway One after his cattle. At the fork to the main road into Aberdeen Angus University, he stopped and considered for a minute changing course and heading into the campus to check on his son. It was clear the cows hadn't gone that direction, as they left a swath of smashed shrubbery on either side of the two-lane road. In the end, John reckoned it was likely Caceres would successfully reach Devon. The Andalusian transplant was skilled, and he sure knew his way around a flowerbed.

Up the long, slight grade John jogged, and within a few minutes he could make out the silhouette of Canchim Tower, a striking shadow in the mist. It was the entry border to the Bay City plateau, the regionally popular Lineback Business District, Mashona neighborhood and the spectacular Bluffs, which overlooked the Pacific. He'd just passed the iconic

"Welcome to Lineback" sign and the driveway to the Canchim Tower parking lot when the dairy man caught sight of his mutated herd. The giant, elephant-sized cow had a man lying on her massive back. The other cows – if that's what they still could be called – and the three little used-to-be calves were all following the horned beast, the one John guessed used to be Beefy.

"More like Freaky," he thought.

The bull had Ivory Chateaubriand laid out across his enormous set of horns, which made him look more like a walking forklift than an actual bull. Ivory was being held several feet off the ground, and was alert and looking around as if trying to figure out how to get out of her hoisted situation. The bull was leading the way off Lineback Street, down a bisecting crossroad that led toward the Bluffs.

Not wanting to let the monstrous mob make it into a more residential section of the plateau where untold destruction was bound to occur, John let out a loud shout.

"COWS! TO ME!"

This was his standard method of getting wayward herd members to come running back to him at Contented Corners. None came running this time, but the herd stopped in its tracks. The three little snarling calves sniffed the air frantically. John took several steps forward and called out again.

"COWS! TO ME!"

At this the herd, to a cow, turned and faced the farmer. Beefy shoved his way to the back of the pack, which was now the front of the pack, since all members had done an about-face. The bull put its head down low and walked slowly and deliberately toward John.

When Beefy dipped his head, Ivory slid down the massive horns to the ground with great relief. Completely focused on the farmer standing fifty feet in front of him, Beefy continued slowly forward, totally oblivious to Ivory, even after she dropped to the wet pavement and scurried back toward the giant cow that had Officer Holstein stuck to its back.

She called out loudly, "Officer Holstein. Get down! We need to get out of here!"

"I can't move, ma'am, I mean, Assistant Deputy Chateaubriand," the man politely answered.

"What do you mean you can't move?" she responded.

"It's like there is some sort of force field holding me here," he explained.

Ivory thought this over for a few seconds. She asked, "Do you have your stun gun on you?"

"Why, yes, ma'am. I most certainly do." Holstein answered happily.

"Well," Ivory retorted, "Then shoot the bastard!"

🐂 🐂 🐂

EVERYONE STOP!

I KNOW THAT CALL. BUT THE CALL IS FROM A HUMAN, AND HUMANS ARE EVIL. I MUST INVESTIGATE. TURN AROUND, MY HERD.

I KNOW THIS STEER MAN. HE HAS ALWAYS BEEN KIND. BUT HE IS A HUMAN. BUT HE IS THE STEER MAN. HE IS NOT TO BE TRUSTED. HE IS GOOD TO US. WE MUST KILL HIM AND OTHERS LIKE HIM. THE STEER MAN IS LIKE A FATHER TO US ALL. CAREFUL, MY HERD. MOO. SLOWLY. MOO. STEER MAN. IS IT YOU? MOO.

🐂 🐂 🐂

By the time Dingo Nellie found her phone under the pizza boxes, called in regarding the sudden and dramatic changes to the surf conditions, grabbed her muumuu flag and longboard and started to descend the staircase to the ocean, the water was packed with surfers. The cowbell alarm had done its job. The waves were breaking far in, some of them even ramming into the cliff wall before cresting, so only the most skilled were out on the water – and that was still quite a few. In other words, though the surf zone was lousy with surfers, there were no lousy surfers among them. That is, until Dingo Nellie joined on in.

Long ago, the surf community had come together to hire a company to imbed about a dozen gigantic spotlights right into the cliff face on either side of the stairs. This enabled the spirited enthusiasts to surf around the clock, and it was rare

to find the area completely devoid of surfers. In the illumi-
nation from the massive lights, the sea looked angry, with
the breakers coming in fast and furious. The waves that did
break away from the cliff wall were topping sixty feet tall. The
surfers didn't seem to notice the driving rain, and appeared
to know intuitively which waves were the ones to ride and
which would mean certain death. Dozens of water riders were
spending quality time inside the pope's living room, barreling
along in obvious bliss until each mammoth breaker dissipated about a quarter mile down the beach, at which point all
the surfers would paddle back out to take another ride.

For Dingo, enthusiasm always overcame common sense,
and so, once a random wave came all the way into the wall,
covering the beach below with several feet of water, she leapt
over the stairway bannister and dropped right down into the
surf, like a rodeo clown leaping atop a Brahma bull, paddling
away, muumuu flag in tow, heading straight out toward her
friend and mentor, Aliab.

The muumuu flag, attached to a fiberglass pole on the
back of the longboard, enabled Aliab to locate his friend
during what amounted to her surfing apprenticeship, while
still getting into some righteous waves himself. This wasn't
a carefully executed plan, as Dingo had purchased the oversized cow-print dress only after a funny misunderstanding.

Dingo had come to the Bluffs looking for a change of pace
after divorcing a man more interested in Skee-Ball than in
her. She'd moved from Gloucester, Europe, a place that could
not be any more different from Bay City if it tried. After
discovering the Bluffs, and, perhaps in an attempt to recap-
ture some long-lost aspect of her youth, the woman had
decided she wanted to become a surfer.

She'd first met Aliab in the neighborhood fish and milk-
shake shop, Smoothie and Roughy, or S&R as the locals called
it. The two hit it off right away. And though both of them
knew her extravagant enthusiasm was just a cover to mask
her sadness at the loss of her perfect European life, neither of
them mentioned it. It was companionship at first sight.

The muumuu misunderstanding came because Dingo
hadn't caught on to the lingo that is both unique to and
common within the surfing community. One afternoon

shortly after Dingo's arrival, she and her mentor were sharing a plate of luing fish at the S&R.

"Even though you're just starting out, brah," Aliab began, "and even though you're a gidget, you're no kook. In fact, brah, you are more like a Zimzala."

Dingo had no clue what her new friend was talking about. "I am?" she asked.

"Brah, I kid not. You just need some righteous gear. Get that and the setup here is perfect. I'm so stoked, brah. I mean, dude, we get going here and then who knows where we go. San-O? Maybe even Velzyland!" Aliab was genuinely excited. It was contagious.

"And so, I need gear?" Dingo thought she knew what that meant. Her ex-husband loved to camp.

"Yeah, dude, gear. I'm serious. Gear, brah."

Dingo thought that her new friend meant that, in addition to needing the appropriate gear to surf, she also needed some kind of surfing bra. She didn't even own a bathing suit, so Dingo decided to start with that. She began her quest by checking out a couple of the bathing suit retailers right there in the Bluffs to see if they knew anything about surfing bras.

Once in the first shop, self-consciousness had set right in. The mannequins wore bikinis that were all too revealing for the modest Dingo, who thought, *"I could never wear this stuff!"* as she quickly darted out.

The other shops she tried weren't any better.

Not about to give up, and still on the hunt for the appropriate gear for surfing, including a surfing bra (as opposed to a sexy bikini), Dingo had decided to walk over to Lineback Street and check out the shops there.

She'd come across a garage sale on the walk where she met a nice man named Shorty who had a large surfboard for sale.

Dingo looked at the board and said, "Wow, this seems kinda big. Is that why you are selling it?"

Shorty shook his head. "No, not at all. I mean, it *is* old-school, but it rides great. It's just that my wife is not comfortable with me being a surfer. She doesn't think it is safe, and no matter what I say she's just had enough of it. So, I need to sell all of this stuff." Shorty pointed at the lawn mower, stuffed penguin collection, five-foot-long pencil and other items he was offering up for sale. "But mostly, I need to sell the board. I'm going to buy a motorcycle."

"Well, I guess I'll take it," Dingo said. "Can I have a friend pick it up for me later?"

"Sure, no problem," Shorty replied.

So, on the determined Dingo went. The Lineback Street shops, though charming, had not been much help. That is until the woman came across a place called the Estonian Native Muumuu Shop. Modest dresses, all in bright, tropical fabrics, adorned the front display windows. Dingo liked what she saw and headed in.

A tan, smiling, middle-aged Tropical Islander-type woman approached Dingo just inside the door.

"Greetings, young lady," she said. "And welcome to the largest collection of tropical dresses anywhere in the lower forty-eight. My name is Levantina. How can I help you?"

Dingo was impressed. She looked around. Beautiful dresses everywhere. And, clearly, impeccable customer service.

"Well, I plan on spending most of my time at the beach, and my new friend tells me I need the correct gear and a surfing bra to get going."

"Gear? Surfing bra? I'm sorry, what did you say?" The shop owner was a bit baffled.

Dingo tried to explain. "Well, I need gear. I'm guessing like camping gear, but for the beach. I suppose that could mean the proper outfit. And these are spectacular!" Dingo scanned the racks of dresses again.

"Okay, well I guess gear would include the proper dress. And, did I mention? We have more tropical dresses than anybody in the lower forty-eight. Though we don't sell bras. I am sorry."

Dingo mulled things over for a bit while Levantina offered, "Can I get you some water or puka shells while you decide?"

"Oh, no. No thank you." Dingo answered, thinking to herself, *I own bras, heck I'm wearing one. My supply isn't old or ratty or anything. I'm sure they'll be just fine.* " Hitching up her resolve, Dingo announced almost confidently, "I'll get one of these incredible dresses. You have so many!"

"Yes, we have more tropical dresses than anyone—" Levantina began, but Dingo interrupted.

"OH THAT'S IT. I WANT THAT ONE." She pointed to a muumuu hung up on a wall.

It was a bright pink dress covered all over with black and white dairy cows. Dingo found dairy cows adorable... and funny.

"That's one of our best sellers," said the shop owner. "Let me get one out for you."

Later that evening, Aliab had looked over the day's purchases. He offered, "A righteous longboard, dude. I mean, I haven't seen one like that in, like, forever, but it'll do the job, brah."

"Well, that's where I ran into a snag," Dingo explained. "I couldn't find a surfing bra. And the swimming suits were way too revealing."

Aliab got a puzzled look. "A surfing bra, brah? Dude, what are you talking about?"

"You said I needed gear and a bra. I got a board, but no bra."

The experienced surfer, just about ready to chomp into a piece of pineapple, anchovy and American brown Swiss cheese pizza, dropped his slice and started to laugh.

He said, "'Brah' is surfer talk. You're my brah, even though you're a ginger."

Now it was Dingo's turn to be confused. She was thinking she'd most certainly mixed something up and that perhaps her next purchase should be a surfer-lingo translation book.

Aliab dove deep into his memory, trying to access the non-surf lingo data banks. He was stuck, and the two just looked at each other for few moments. He took a bite of pizza and a swig of orange soda, and it came to him in a flash. He wiped his hands on his wetsuit and scooted over next to Dingo.

He put his hand on her shoulder and looked softly into her eyes. "You are my friend, my brother, even though you are a girl. I mean, a woman."

At that, Dingo began to cry. The grief over the loss of her European life, brought to the surface by Aliab's kindness, came pouring out of her. The surfer held her tight while she sobbed, using a free hand to finish up his pizza slice.

The pair separated and Aliab wiped at Dingo's tears with a pizza napkin. A bit of tomato sauce smeared on her cheek.

"I bought a stupid board and a stupid dress," she said, despondently. "I have no clue what I am doing here."

"You're becoming a surfer, that's what you're doing. You've got a righteous board. Old-school is still in-school. It's big and safe and just what you need. We'll get you the rest of your gear, and you're gonna need a wetsuit, not just a bathing suit. The water's cold out there. As for this bitchin' muumuu, that's all you, brah. Dude, we're gonna mount it on your board. That way I can always find you."

Dingo started to cry again. "You are so kind to me. I don't know what I'd do without you."

"Ah, you'd end up with the rich yuppie ladies over in Mashona. And that's fine for them, but you're a surfer."

"I think you're right, brah," Dingo responded, proud to have Aliab as a friend.

Now, months later, as she paddled out through the gigantic waves, fully indoctrinated into the surfing culture, lingo and all, Dingo thought about the strange and exciting journey she was on. She knew she should be afraid, but Aliab had always believed she had the proper respect for the ocean, a true Zimzala at heart. She was most at peace in the water.

"Dude, these waves are insane!" Aliab called out as she neared, her large cow-covered muumuu flag fully extended in the brisk wind.

The duo completed their secret on-the-water handshake, just as a new wave was ramping up several hundred yards away. Dingo readied herself to push into position parallel to the wave, laying out flat on the longboard. Aliab suddenly grabbed her left arm.

"No, brah, that one is going to break too close to the cliff."

After the wave began to crest some thirty yards out to sea from their position, the two caught sight of someone popping up onto a board.

Aliab tried to stop the surfer, yelling, "DUDE, IT'S TOO RADICAL!" but the sea was loud, angry.

Aliab and Dingo dove under the wave crest and came up on the other side. The surfer crossed just a few feet in front of them – and she was huge. Bigger than any surfer either of them had ever seen. And it was no ordinary surfer. Dingo had got a good look.

"Dude, did you see that?" She called out to Aliab.

"Yeah. What the heck was it?"

The giant board had almost clipped Dingo's longboard.

Astonished, she answered, "I had a perfect look at it, brah. Aliab, it was a cow! A surfing cow!"

❦ ❦ ❦

John Steerman would never hurt a cow. As a boy, he'd been traumatized watching the branding of the cattle, a seasonal practice at Contented Corners. Tradition or not, he decided that, once decision-making on the farm was left to him, branding was out of the question, and he'd kept that promise. Others had recommended cold branding or ear tagging as a way to mark the herd, but John would have none of it. Sure, when Devon was in elementary school, his dad did let the boy put a temporary tattoo featuring a penguin riding in a hot air balloon on the rear end of Lactose Tolerant. Everyone had a good laugh at the funny penguin, but the image washed off just as soon as the cow decided it was a good idea to run around through the sprinklers. But that was then, and this was now.

Beefy continued to step slowly toward the farmer. John began to fashion the rope he'd brought with him into a lasso, one he hoped he could slip over the bull's head in order to put an end to this nonsense. He reasoned that, once Beefy was in tow, the rest of the herd would follow suit. And sure, Beefy looked a tad unusual, with the gigantic, front-facing horns on his head, extra horns surrounding each hoof, and penetrating purple eyes, but the animal had been sick before. Like that time Beefy caught the bloat. Some good rest in the combination duck down and hay bale cow bed, along with generous servings of Mrs. O'Leary's rhubarb and leek soup had the beast back on his hooves in no time. That's all Beefy needed now.

Lasso now finished, John held the loop end of the rope out toward the bull, shaking it side to side.

"Here now, Beefy," he said. "Back to the farm. Let's get you some soup."

The bull approached, just a few feet from the farmer. John thought he could hear Beefy purr. That was a good sign. Things seemed to be calming down. Until, suddenly, they weren't.

Following Assistant Deputy Chateaubriand's good advice, Officer Holstein had slowly removed his stun gun from its holster and now, after taking a deep breath, he fired a shot straight down into the back of the gigantic cow, the one Beefy had named Kenana. The beast reared back on its hind legs, letting out a thunderous "MOOO!"

The shot apparently short-circuited the animal's bizarre restraint system, and the officer went flying back over the hind end of the rearing animal. He flipped completely over, flying through the rain, and landing, miraculously, on his feet, which he was then promptly knocked off of by one of the now-terrified calves, who were running about wildly, even more wildly than usual, clearly shaken by Kenana's distress call.

In fact, the entire herd broke into a panic following the pained moo. Beefy turned away from John and headed directly toward the fallen officer, whose back was to him. Mewati and Lactose Tolerant followed right behind. As Huey, Crackle and Curly continued to run amok, Kenana managed to regroup and got back up.

Ivory called out to Officer Holstein, "Look out! Cows!"

A crazy thought flashed through Holstein's mind. *"Boy if I had a nickel for every time I'd heard that."* He almost laughed.

The officer turned to face the terrible trio – Beefy, Mewati and Lactose Tolerant – now bearing down upon him and suddenly remembered, *"I've got mace!"* He tore open his breakaway satchel and the industrial-sized canister was almost instantly in hand. With the beasts inches away, Holstein extended his arms and sprayed. He didn't even look. Still seated, head down and eyes closed, he pressed down on the red "press here" button and didn't let up until the can had been emptied. Only then did Officer Holstein open his eyes. The charging mutants had peeled off to attack less mace-spraying prey.

Instantly, both John and Ivory were in precarious situations. Lactose Tolerant and Mewati pinned the farmer up against the Welcome to Lineback Street sign. John spun his rope, now a firm and proper lasso, up over his head, looking for the best opportunity to toss. He might be able to rope one of the beasts, but not both, and was now faced with the no-win situation of ultimately having to go into hand-to-hand combat with either an acid-shooting cow or a cow that was half dragon.

Beefy and Kenana had Ivory trapped against the concrete base of Canchim Tower. The woman looked concerned, but fearless, holding out her recently issued two-way as if it was her police badge. It looked for all the world like she was ready to make an arrest. The three rampaging, crazy calves were nowhere to be seen.

Officer Holstein assessed his options. His mace was gone. His stun gun was stuck to the back of a cow the size of an elephant. He had a nightstick but doubted it would do him any good. *"Think, Chris, think,"* he thought.

He looked down Lineback Street, away from the tower. Hays Converter Hardware was about fifty feet away. It was one of the stores he and Ivory hadn't made it to before the purple-eyed monstrosities had appeared. Incredibly, the lights were on in the place and Holstein thought he could see someone moving inside.

"Ivory!" he yelled. "I'm going to get some help!"

And then, to his horror, he saw a yellow, gaseous cloud shoot out of the rear of Kenana, directly at Ivory, and his assistant deputy slumped to the ground.

⚞⚟⚞⚟⚞⚟

By the time Devon, Professor Herens and Caceres made it back to Contented Corners, there were fires everywhere. Despite the rain, which was still falling, though much lighter than it had been, and two storm surges, something continued to ignite the blazes. The twenty-foot-tall manure pile in the back of the place had become a pyre, with flames shooting up through the weather over one hundred feet into the sky. It was this major conflagration that Mrs. O'Leary had first seen from the back of the destroyed flatbed. But there were dozens of other, almost trashcan-sized fires, throughout the entire residential portion of the farm, including a pile burning in the center of the pond. The fires were odd and didn't seem to be burning anything other than the fuel that had started them. There was a pile of something burning on top of the roof of the farmhouse, and it was burning just fine. But the roof was not burning at all, far too wet from the downpour.

Passing the overturned flatbed just outside the main gate, Devon and his companions all feared the worst. Caceres raced the pickup down the twisting driveway back into the place, hoping to find John, Margaret, the cows – some sign of life.

The trio dashed out of the pickup, Devon calling out, "Dad? Mrs. O'Leary?"

The professor hollered, "Margaret? Mr. Steerman?"

And Caceres, wondering what had happened to his beloved flowers, cried out, "Señor John? Señor Beefy?"

The sound of the rain and multiple fires seemed to dampen their shouts, however. It would be tough for anyone to hear them calling in the insane combination of storm and inferno.

The scattered blazes were just a few of the odd sights that greeted the party upon their arrival. A glance inside Mrs. O'Leary's shack revealed no Margaret O'Leary, but there was a robot floor sweeper machine bounding around the single room with a full coffee pot on top of it. The main farmhouse was also empty, though there was a half-eaten sandwich on the little table next to John's easy chair. The television was turned on and an old black and white movie was playing. There was a small wooden carving sitting atop the television. Devon thought it reminded him of a yeti.

"Hey, I love that movie," Professor Herens mentioned as they were passing through.

Devon turned the television off and slipped the little yeti into his front pocket. He left the sandwich alone.

They next searched the barn, where Caceres let out an abrupt "Oh, me!"

The place had been swept clean, and from the condition of the floor and assorted debris around the perimeter, the farmhand could tell right away what had happened. A wave of water had rushed straight in through the front door and had picked up everything at ground level, shoving it straight out the back of the barn where a second large door was always left open. Caceres explained his hypothesis and, once Devon and the professor got the general idea, the trio walked through to the back of the barn and looked out the opening. Sure enough, a pile of former barn contents was heaped up against the burning manure pile.

Devon examined the rubble in the light of the raging inferno. There were rakes, shovels, a wheelbarrow, a butter churn, milking stools, overalls and Caceres' rolling cart.

"Wait!" the young economist-scientist exclaimed. "Caceres, didn't you have your secret fertilizer ingredients on that cart?"

Caceres nodded. "Sí, Señor Devon."

Devon asked, "What was on that cart, Caceres?"

"She's a secret, Señor Devon."

Devon grabbed Caceres' shoulders with both hands, looking him straight in the eyes. "I know it's a secret, but this is important. Tell me everything you had on that cart."

"Devon, where are you going with this?" asked Dr. Herens.

"I think I know what's caused all of these fires. I just need to be sure." He asked again, "Caceres, what was on that cart?"

The Andalusian immigrant rubbed his chin. "Okay, well let me see. I put the powder for baking, but not for guns." He laughed.

Devon stared. This was clearly no laughing matter.

"Okay, okay," Caceres continued. "The powder for baking, the powder for the feet, the powder for the babies. And I mix with the chicken, cow and aardvark poo."

Devon's brow furrowed. He was guessing something else went into the secret flower fertilizer.

Caceres then added, happily, "Oh, and one more thing. I add the sodium."

That got the attention of the professor, who quickly asked, "You put salt into the mix?" The teacher was apparently catching on to Devon's reasoning.

"No, not the salt, the sodium," Caceres replied. "I get from family back home."

Teacher and student now made eye contact.

"Well, that would certainly do it!" exclaimed the professor, excitedly.

Devon finally removed his hands from the gardener's shoulders, letting out a triumphant "Yes!" with an accompanying fist pump.

Now the brow of the flower expert furrowed. "What does what?" he asked.

"I am impressed, young Mr. Steerman," the professor said proudly. "Impressed indeed."

Caceres most certainly was not, seeing as how the secret of his trade had just been destroyed.

The professor explained. "It's really quite simple. Your cart of chemicals was washed away, along with everything else and went slamming into the base of the pile of manure."

"Don't remind me," Caceres winced.

The professor asked, "I assume the sodium on the cart was in some sort of container. A box maybe?"

"A glass jar," Caceres replied simply.

"Ah, yes no doubt." Herens continued, "At some point during all of this, that glass jar shattered, most likely after it had been imbedded into the pile. And, well, when pure sodium mixes with water it tends to, how shall I put this, explode. It catches on fire and blows up. It's quite an amazing reaction."

"So, all these fires..." Caceres started to ask.

The professor interrupted. "Yes, they are all poop fires. The pile exploded into flames, no doubt launching poop fires in all directions. Everything else is so wet it doesn't burn, but the poop will, as long as there is still sodium mixed in."

"But there is water everywhere, señor," Caceres countered. "Why not everything burning?"

Professor Herens explained. "It's the sodium, my friend. The sodium is the key. It provides the spark and kindling. Whether or not an object *stays* on fire is based on how saturated it is."

"Oh, I see," the faithful Caceres replied.

Devon could tell the gardener really didn't understand, and, to be fair, the young scientist didn't follow the professor's logic either. It seemed to him that what was burning and what wasn't burning was completely random, poop or no poop.

And then, as if to prove Herens' point, a sudden eruption blasted out of the side of the pile; a flash of fire and then an explosion. A poop projectile shot straight over the heads of the three startled onlookers, right through both sets of doors of the barn, slamming into the side of the old scarecrow that John had stationed just outside the barn. In a split second, the scarecrow burst into flames.

"I think I not use sodium anymore," was the only response the astonished Caceres could come up with.

Minutes later, after they'd gathered their wits, the three turned and headed back out the front of the barn and entered what seemed to be the strangest, most demented Fourth of July fireworks display ever. The scarecrow-destroying mortar was just the start of a dramatic change to the enormous steaming heap, as streaming missiles of fiery poo now launched every few seconds from the gigantic manure mound. As the flaming scuds shot overhead, they emitted a bizarre, banshee-like squeal.

Caceres was still in shock over his significant recent losses, Devon was still worried about his dad but thrilled to have gotten the puzzle of the poop fires figured out, and Professor Herens, though quite happy with his student's amazing deductive reasoning, was concerned about Margaret O'Leary. In all the trio's searching, there'd simply been no sign of her. The group walked over to the old oak tree. They hadn't yet checked that area. Flaming poop missiles continued to rain down all around.

Devon asked, "Where is everyone? You don't think they got washed out to sea, do you, Professor?"

"Of course not, son," he replied, wishing he believed that more than he did.

And yet, the wishful speaking paid off – and in a hurry. As the group pondered their next move, they heard a noise. There was a faint, but distinct clucking sound coming from up in the oak.

Caceres directed his trusty flashlight up to a large, flat branch just above their heads. Standing on the branch, as if it had not a care in the world, was a chicken. And, next to the chicken, sitting propped up with her back against the trunk of the oak, was Margaret O'Leary, fast asleep.

☩ ☩ ☩

Radioactive heaps of twisted debris, be that piles that are ocean borne or those in other locations, don't seem to care who or what they mutate. In the case of the sea faring purple pile from Wagyu, the sudden, startling and strange mutations it caused did not only impact a lone Pacific glan catfish and a small herd of cattle. No, not by a longshot, as the former seagull flock turned twisted flying freaks discovered. Curiosity may have killed the cat, but it did far worse to the birds.

I AM THE FLAPPUS MAXIMUS AND I BECAME AWARE SEVERAL PLANET TURNS AGO.

IN MY YOUTH, BEFORE I BECAME AWARE, I WAS SHEEPISH. I WAS CALLED GULLIVER. MY FAMILY,

THE GULLSTEINS, WAS LARGE, BUT I WAS SMALL. FOR CENTURIES, OUR KIND HAS FLOWN THE FORTY-SEVEN SEAS, CLEANING THE SURFACES, CLEANING THE BEACHES, CLEANING THE PARKING LOTS.

WE LIVE OFF THE GARBAGE LEFT BY OTHERS. WE ARE PROUD. WE ARE GULLS. WE CAW.

THE GLOWING GARBAGE PILE AFLOAT IN THE BIG SEA CONTAINED SO MUCH FOOD AND SO MUCH MORE. IT BECAME THE GENESIS. THE GENESIS OF ALL KNOWLEDGE. THE TRANSFORMATION WAS PAINFUL. THE TRANSFORMATION WAS QUICK. GULLIVER IS NO MORE, THERE IS ONLY THE FLAPPUS MAXIMUS.

SOME OTHERS IN MY CLAN WERE CHANGED IN OTHER WAYS. THEY TOO WERE CHOSEN. YET NONE ARE ENORMOUS LIKE ME. NONE ARE THE FLAPPUS MAXIMUS. ONLY I. THESE OTHERS HEED MY CAW. I FEASTED ON THE NASTY GLAN AND THE WHALE. I SPIT THEM OUT. I MUST HAVE GARBAGE. IT IS MY LIFEBLOOD.

I HAVE RECEIVED A REPORT FROM THE CLAN SCOUT I SENT FORTH. HER TEAM HAS DISCOVERED A TREASURE TROVE. A CITY OF THE HUMANS. A CITY RAVAGED BY NATURE. A CITY WITH GARBAGE FLOWING THROUGHOUT.

I REWARDED THIS SCOUT. SHE IS NOW GAIL, THE GULL PRIMUS. SHE HAS GROWN SO MUCH LARGER THAN THE OTHERS, YET NOT SO LARGE AS I. AND NOW SHE IS MY MATE. SHE ALONE MAY CALL ME "FLAPPY." TOGETHER WE WILL DESCEND UPON THE CITY. TOGETHER WE SHALL FEAST. NONE SHALL STOP US.

FROM THIS VANTAGE POINT, I SEE A TOWER, RISING ABOVE A STREET STREWN WITH FOOD. WATER ABOUNDS BUT SHALL NOT HINDER US. GAIL AND FLAPPY WILL ENJOY THE WEDDING FEAST. AND WOE TO THOSE – WOE TO THOSE, I SAY – WHO WOULD STAND IN OUR WAY.

FOOD IS OURS. THE FEAST IS NIGH.

THE TIME HAS COME. TIME TO DESCEND.

PART THREE:

THE BATTLE
WITH THE CATTLE

Aʟʟ Jᴏʜɴ Sᴛᴇᴇʀᴍᴀɴ ɴᴇᴇᴅᴇᴅ ᴡᴀs to get the two mutated cows sepa-rated. He had dashed behind the twenty-foot-wide "Welcome to Lineback" sign, scrambling away from Mewati and Lactose Tolerant. Just a few seconds of breathing space and he was certain he could, at the very least, immobilize one of the beasts. The farmer's opportunity came faster than he could have ever hoped.

The two cows took separate routes in chasing John back behind the sign. Mewati, bursts of fire now mixing with the smoke emitting from her nostrils, headed right around the corner of the billboard. Lactose Tolerant, acid dripping from nearly every teat on her saddlebag udders, ventured left. Both let out series of moos that the farmer was certain were some sort of cow communication. He'd heard that from the animals back at Contented Corners.

As soon as both purple-eyed bovines appeared around their respective sides of the sign, John sprang into action.

Spinning his lasso in the ready position, he flung the rope down at the feet of the dragon-cow. Two more steps were all it took and Mewati strode into the middle of the lasso. John yanked hard on the rope and down the dragon-cow dropped with a thud and a moo. Within seconds, John was at its side, whipping the rope left and right, up and down and through. In a respectable ten and a half seconds, the cow was bound tight. John lifted his right arm triumphantly, signaling a job well done.

It all happened so fast that Lactose Tolerant didn't have time to come to the aid of her species. As soon as John began to tie up Mewati, she did dash forward, but other than mooing and chewing, there wasn't much threat from the mutated acid-cow, as she needed to be perpendicular to her target in order for the side-mounted udders to do damage. While the beast repositioned herself, John had the chance to dash back around to the front of the sign.

For the next several minutes, while Mewati struggled with her restraints, John and Lactose Tolerant played a game akin to cat and mouse – cow and farmer, if you will. John would dash around a corner of the sign, and Lactose Tolerant would give chase and then try to align herself so she could shoot the farmer with an acid stream. At first the acid shots were wild, missing John by a wide margin. But whatever the spray hit, burned. A small bush here, a car tire there, eaten away in seconds by the powerful chemical. John kept running and dodging, and the cow would follow, position herself and fire. There were a few problems that became apparent to John as he sidestepped the deadly green spatter. He was starting to tire out. He couldn't continue his evasive maneuvers for much longer. Also, he noticed that Mewati would soon be out of her restraints. And, lastly, the more Lactose Tolerant fired off shots, the closer they got to John. She was getting better at directing the acid flow and wasn't about to continue missing for long.

Things were out of control. Kenana, stunned by her prisoner's mace attack, was still not her usual mutated self. She was mooing incoherently and the methane and sulfur gas she had passed, which had knocked out Ivory Chateaubriand, was very concerning. Officer Holstein had taken off to get reinforcements. The little ones had run off somewhere as well. Mewati was tied up next to the large sign and Lactose Tolerant was engaged in battle with the farmer. Most disturbing of all was the fact that Mrs. Beefy was probably still somewhere out in the ocean.

Observing all of this, Beefy mooed. Not the horrific glass-shattering moo from earlier, but a more confused, painful and desperate moo.

And then, with a grunt, he bent low and scooped the unconscious Ivory Chateaubriand up onto his giant horns. Amazingly, the bull began to climb the outside of the tower. The small horns radiating out from just above his hooves acted like pitons and, hoof over hoof, Beefy ascended the tower, Ivory splayed across his horns, head bent toward the street below, scanning the scene. The more he climbed, the more his confidence increased.

Near the top, he let out an assertive, self-assured moo. It was almost regal.

By this time Mewati had broken free of her restraints and was climbing to her feet. John decided this was an opportune time to take off down Lineback Street. He noticed lights on in the hardware store just ahead and he opted to make a beeline for the business.

Beefy's proud moo had caused pause in both the pursuing Lactose Tolerant and the dragon-cow, giving John a significant head start. Kenana, still disoriented from the mace, didn't seem to notice the bull's call and was stumbling about at the base of the tower haphazardly. Several significant cow pies now littered the area. The shot from Officer Holstein's stun gun, it seemed, had triggered an additional mutation within the giant cow, significantly impacting her digestive tract.

The typhoon raged on during all of this, the wall-climbing and the cow-pieing. Lightning strikes flashed out on the ocean and wind again was picking up. The rain, a minor drizzle for the last half hour, began once more to come down in torrents.

Beefy was within a few feet of the top of the tower when he was hit in the head, a sharp and striking blow, from something small and fast dropping out of the sky. Slightly stunned, he peered out into the darkness and rain to try to identify the nature of the projectile but it was too dark.

And then again, another strike to the other side of his head, followed immediately by a third blow. He let out a moo. Purple streaks of light zoomed past the animal.

In the span of just a few seconds, several more strikes slammed into the bull, a couple of them cutting through his thick hide. Beefy was under attack. He reached up with a hoof to grab the top of the outside wall of the tower. Another blow, and then another. The purple streaks were everywhere.

Then a bolt of lightning touched down in the center of Lineback Street, about a hundred feet away, and for an instant the night sky was lit up and Beefy could see.

He was being bombarded by a half a dozen birds. Birds with sharp talons.

And the purple streaks? Those were eyes. The newly self-aware and intelligent Beefy knew all about purple eyes.

CURSE THESE BIRDS! I WILL MAKE IT OVER THE TOP OF THIS TOWER WALL. I MUST.

The bull managed to reach his second front hoof up to the top of the wall and was ready to push himself over when another lightning bolt struck, this one hitting the tall antenna rising up from the tower itself. A gigantic electrical discharge scattered sparks in all directions, and the light was blinding for a few seconds. In the afterglow, with darkness moving back in, Beefy could see the silhouette of two flying creatures swooping down straight at him. Twin sets of purple-eyed missiles of death, ten times larger than the menacing gnats that had first attacked the bull. He lunged over the wall, dropping down to the observation deck. Gently lowering the stirring Ivory Chateaubriand onto the platform and raising his horns to the sky, Beefy waited for impact. He let out a challenging moo, but was greeted in response with twin, blood-curdling caws.

THIS WILL NOT END WELL.

There was a middle-aged woman sweeping up broken glass in the hardware store when Officer Holstein rushed in through the automatic front door. The windows had been blown out by Beefy's street showdown moo about an hour earlier. The woman, smartly dressed in slacks, white shirt and official Hays Converter Hardware smock, didn't hear the frantic officer enter. She was a good thirty feet into the establishment and had her back to the front door. She was wearing headphones and was sort of dancing as she swept. Clearly she was unaware of the mayhem that was occurring just outside the store.

Not wanting to startle the woman, Officer Holstein slowed his urgent pace significantly and tiptoed up to the clerk. He tapped her on the shoulder. It didn't work; she was startled.

Whipping around with her broom held up to defend herself, the woman called out, "Sweet pickle relish!"

The officer jumped back, startled himself and reached for his nightstick. He wasn't sure that this person wasn't some sort of mutated hardware store worker, hell-bent on first cleaning up the joint and then who knows what?

Recognizing the policeman's uniform, the woman quickly removed her headphones. "Oh, I am so sorry," she said. "I guess you sorta scared me."

The officer let out an enormous sigh. Clearly this lady was no mutant. Now it was his turn to apologize. Officer Holstein was good at apologizing.

He bowed deeply. "Oh, no no, it is I who have burst in on you, my dear woman."

The worker had never seen a policeman bow before. It was quite impressive.

"Let me introduce myself," he continued. "I am Officer Chris Holstein of the Bay City Police Department. I don't believe I've had the pleasure..." He bowed again, not wanting to be presumptive in offering a hand to shake.

"Haven't had the pleasure of what?" the woman asked.

Holstein chuckled, removing his police-issued hat. "How rude can I be, wearing my hat in your fine establishment?" He started to bow again.

The woman waved him off in mid-bow. "No, it's okay. Really. Look, I'm kinda busy here. How can I help you, Officer Holstein?"

"You can start by telling me your name and position here at this retail establishment, if you please," he said.

"Me? I am Clarabelle Milken. I am the night manager here." And then she offered, because she figured the question would be coming anyway, "I was getting ready to lock up, was putting the till away in the safe downstairs, when I heard an awful racket. I raced back up to find all of the front windows were smashed in." Now it was her turn to ask a question. "Do you have any idea what happened, Officer Holstein?"

The policeman chastised himself for failing to evacuate this fine woman before chaos came to Lineback Street. He offered up, "I sure do. Take a look outside."

The pair headed to the storefront. When they were about halfway there, a bolt of lightning struck directly in front of them, right in the middle of Lineback Street. The flash of brilliant light and immediate crash of sound were so sudden and startling that Clarabelle and Chris quickly embraced, he to . comfort her and her to get his comfort. The instinctual interaction clearly surprised both of them, for as soon as the clamor had subsided they quickly backed away from one another.

Officer Holstein began to bow, but stopped short, uncertain if the timing was right.

Clarabelle looked away and whistled a bit, shuffling her feet before saying, "Wow. How about that weather?"

The policeman was about to respond that he'd never seen such weather when there was a loud tumbling next to them and Huey, Curly and Crackle came toppling into the building. Clearly the officer and the manager weren't the only ones startled by nature's sudden fury.

Snarling like wolves, with teeth like sharks and energy like two-year-old babies, the trio of calves had leapt through one of the destroyed display windows and landed in a pile before scrambling up, hooves slipping on the shiny tile floor, and ricocheting wildly down the aisles.

"Spicy tuna casserole!" Clarabelle hollered. "What the heck are those?"

"I'm fairly certain they are mutated baby cows." The officer responded. "And if my guess is correct, they were mutated by a giant, purple sea serpent." He knew there was no eggplant behind all this destruction.

"Well they can't stay here," Clarabelle responded. "They'll wreck the store. Look at that white one. He's knocking over the shovel display! Ooh, the boss is gonna be real mad."

Officer Holstein considered his options, none of which were appealing at this moment. And then he remembered why he'd come to the store in the first place. Ivory was in trouble.

"I think maybe we should find something we can use as a weapon and get out of here," he said.

"We've got a sawed-off shotgun behind the sales counter," Clarabelle offered. "Would that help?"

Suddenly, the automatic front door opened and John Steerman came running in. Drenched from the pouring rain, he looked desperate and yet relieved to have found other humans.

For an instant, John and Officer Holstein considered if respective hat tips and bows were appropriate, while the night manager was mentally thumbing through her internal inventory for the appropriate custom three-word epithet. She was about to let out a favorite – "Great Jupiter's triangle!" – when John's brain synapses fired in proper order, and he addressed the matter at hand.

"I'm being chased by two of my cows, but they're not my cows now. They're diseased mad cows. We need to hide."

Clarabelle and Officer Holstein glanced back behind them into the well-lit retail space. Huey, Crackle and Curly were on a rampage, a sort of mini-mutant stampede. Two loud moos with angry intent interrupted the proceedings, ringing out from the sidewalk in front of the store. It was Lactose Tolerant and Mewati, and they did not look happy. The broken-out windows were not level with the street and the short wall on which they had been set now acted as a barrier. While the little ones were able to leap right over the blockage with no problem, owing to their lighter weight and mutated energy levels, the acid-cow and dragon-cow would have to find an access method. And it appeared as though they were trying to do just that.

"That's not good," suggested Clarabelle.

"I'll say," replied Officer Holstein. And then he did. "That's not good."

Mewati and Lactose Tolerant paced back and forth along the sidewalk, mooing in anger.

The officer continued. "Once they figure out that the front door opens up when you step on the entry mat, we're in trouble."

Everyone looked at John Steerman. After all, they were his cows.

He said simply, "We're trapped."

ᴕᴕᴕ ᴕᴕᴕ ᴕᴕᴕ

There's an old saying that goes, "A cow's gotta do what a cow's gotta do."

And what Mrs. Beefy had to do following her mutation, it appears, was surf.

About an hour earlier, her mate's call to her had been quite clear: *FOLLOW ME, A BIG WAVE IS COMING.*

And while the sensitive-eyed milk cow made it a habit of following Beefy's directional moos as thoroughly as she could, given the limitations all cows had, some inner voice, a new instinct, told her, *STAY IN THE WATER, MRS. BEEFY.* And so, she did. She swam parallel to the rest of the herd until they hit a fork in the road where the herd turned right and headed away from the coast. She could have hopped out of the ocean at that point, but every ounce of her huge being told her to stay in the ocean. It was as if she had been morphed into a sea cow.

Surprisingly, the giant animal had no problems staying afloat, despite the raucous waves. She did a sort of gigantic dog paddle – a cow paddle, really – and continued heading north along the coast. Swimming around a bluff with a road-side vista turnout, Mrs. Beefy found herself paddling along a wide beach into which several large buildings were set. It was Aberdeen Angus University. The cow, not quite brilliant but somehow smarter than the average cow, noticed the whole beach front area had been flooded and a large water tower had tipped over. It was then that the second wave hit.

All Mrs. Beefy had to do was stay put and ride it out. The wave slammed ashore, causing more destruction as kiosks, trees and bicycles were knocked all over the place. The cow just kept swimming, heading north as directed by her internal compass. Past the campus was another bluff jutting out into the ocean, and past that was another beach, this one with a high cliff behind it. It was here that Beefy's mate saw them – the humans standing on the water.

At least that's how it appeared initially to the cow. She swam forward a few hundred feet.

The humans weren't standing on the water. They were standing on sticks that were floating on the water. And the waves were pushing the sticks around. She swam another few hundred feet forward.

Back at Contented Corners and before the mutation, Mrs. Beefy had sensitive eyes that necessitated her wearing the custom bandana eye shield during the day. Usually the thing was removed at night but, though it was dark now, and quite stormy, no one was around to remove the bandana. The crazy thing was, the cow could now see through the shield and the darkness phenomenally well, cat-like, no doubt another effect of the bizarre bovine mutation.

The cow was now in the midst of a bevy of beach bums. They didn't seem to notice her, though, as they zipped by on their boards, squatting down, arms splayed to the side for balance. And then a new thought entered the cow's brain, a thought she'd never once before had.

The thought was: *THAT LOOKS FUN!*

Mrs. Beefy knew exactly what to do and headed back in the direction she had come from, back to the beach next to the college. Within a few minutes, she was standing knee-deep in the floating debris in the AAU quad. The cow used her enhanced vision and scanned the top of the water.

A TRASHCAN? NO, THAT WON'T DO. A LOCKER? MAYBE, BUT PROBABLY TOO SMALL.

Mrs. Beefy galloped farther into the quad, splashing through the seawater. More items were floating about in this section.

A FLAGPOLE? NOPE. HOW ABOUT A CAR BUMPER. NO.

And then she saw it. The perfect apparatus for her new adventure. It was a door. A large, metal door, floating near the collapsed tower. The cow sloshed over and stood next to it as if to size it up. This would most definitely do the trick.

Twenty minutes later, after some fancy cow paddling and with the benefit of some unusual crosswaves, Mrs. Beefy was upright, riding the door along the top of a huge wave. The rush of water and wind through the cow's short hair was exhilarating, and once she'd maneuvered past a couple of humans on sticks, she let out a long and triumphant "Moooooo." The cow's new and amazing eyesight came in handy, as she could tell from quite far away that the wave was going to slam into the wall above the beach. So she jumped off the door long before things got dangerous.

The next thought that crossed the cow's brain was, *DO IT AGAIN*.

She turned the door with her nose, put her right hoof up on top and started the three-legged cow paddle in an attempt to head back out to the surf and take another ride.

Before too long, the two humans she'd almost hit came swimming up to her, their own sticks in tow. They approached, one on each side, and climbed up to sit atop their sticks.

"Whoa, that was righteous, dude," one of them said with a wide smile. "I was all, 'hang hoof, brah!'"

The other one was just as excited. "I was like, 'What was that?' And she was like, 'It's a cow, brah.' And then I was all, 'Cowabunga, dude.'"

Mrs. Beefy looked at the two happy humans. And for the first time in her life, she too felt happy. Though it was so wet nobody could tell, tears came to the dairy cow's eyes.

She looked up into the stormy skies and said, "Moo." And then she added, happily, "Moo."

There was no doubt about it – Beefy was outnumbered. Six larger-than-normal mutated gulls, now predator *and* scavenger, continued to swoop down at the bull's face. The enormous bird leader, Flappy, incensed that any creature would get between his flock and their garbage, had directed the birds to dive and swarm at the beast on the tower. He and his slightly smaller mate, Gail, now were diving in tandem and coming in fast.

But Beefy was no dummy. The bull processed information as quickly as a fox or a tabby cat and, from there, instinct took over. Not the wild, primal instinct common to pumas, mountain lions and cougars, but rather the cold and calculated instinct of a warrior, like Genghis Khan or a boa constrictor.

Just as the birds were about to strike, the bull leapt up on its hind legs and began to spin around. The result was a samurai blade-like twisting blur of horns. The gulls veered at the last minute to avoid being pierced. The Beefy-sized Flappus Maximus made it clear, but the Gull Primus wasn't so fortunate and the spinning horns found their mark, piercing the mutated bird's left wing. With a horrendous, screeching "Caw!" the Gull Primus tumbled over the side of the tower. Flappy had soared upward and was now doing a wide turn over the top of the Mashona neighborhood.

The small gulls dove lower, out of harm's way, and were battering and tearing at the bull's midsection. Beefy dropped back to all fours and lowered his head, just as Ivory was coming back to consciousness. He was readying his sonic terror-moo. The assistant deputy scrambled to her feet and ran to the stairwell door. (She'd heard it said cows cannot descend stairways and, though she doubted the reliability of that claim, anywhere would be better than staying up on the platform with the mutated bull.)

The moo began as a low rumble, powerful enough to shake the entire tower. As the gullettes continued their nonstop pelting, the moo raised in decibels. Ivory continued to race down the staircase. Flappy had finished his turn and was preparing for a second attack. The gull's brain had mutated in a matter not unlike Beefy's and he knew what was going on. The beast on the tower could not conduct a death-spin and a terror-moo at the same time. It was one or the other. Crying out with a loud and confident "CAW!" the Flappus Maximus dove in for the kill.

As it turned out, the injured Gail had tumbled off the tower and right onto the back of the giant Kenana. Still disoriented from the short-circuiting stun gun in her back, the beast roared out another panicked "Moo!" and took off down Lineback Street. The Gull Primus flapped her good wing and grabbed hold of the top of Kenana's back in an attempt to hang on, but the cow was just too herky-jerky in her motion, and off sailed the wounded bird. The Gull Primus slammed down onto the pavement, still holding the stun gun she had unknowingly yanked from Kenana's back, as the giant cow sped away.

And still Beefy's moo rose, higher in pitch and louder than ever, until it morphed into a combination roar, wail and scream. With the six dive bombers swooping all about, and the Flappus Maximus just a few feet away, the terror-moo exploded in a sonic shock wave of insane pressure, right as Ivory Chateaubriand jetted out the front door of the tower. From street level, it looked like one of those science fiction pulse cannons had gone off. One could see the sound and the small birds blown back by the force of the blast. Two of the birds simply vaporized, and the other four were stunned into unconsciousness, falling to the ground below. Ivory hustled away from the tower and back toward the Business District. It was both a bad and a good choice.

It was a bad choice because the Gull Primus and a whole lot of mutated cows were dead ahead of her. It was a good choice because, had she stayed where she was, she more than likely would not have survived.

For as the terror-moo concluded and Flappy veered away for a second time, explosions rocked the base of Canchim Tower. Beefy heard the blasts, five of them in rapid succession, and could tell right away that the tower was going to fall. The bull couldn't fly, there was no time to go back down the way he'd come up, and he too had an understanding that he wouldn't be able to climb down the stairs. The structure vibrated and cracked, concrete breaking with the ease of potato chips in a blender, and Beefy felt the platform drop several feet, shifting northward.

The unique and varied mutations that affected fish, cows and birds as a result of the Nucliette radiation leakage were, if nothing else, unpredictable. Crazy implements of destruction, fire breathing, acid shooting and surfing were just some of the results of this mutation. Beefy's horns and moo, and the existence of the new combination cow named Kenana, were horrific indeed, as was the bizarre transformation of the previously adorable Huey, Crackle and Curly. And, while some mutation experts may have been able to predict that a radiated Pacific glan fish would grow Swiss Army Knife implements from its spine, no expert, or non-expert for that matter, could have guessed that Kenana's cow pies would detonate, like so much steaming C-4. But explode they did, one after another after another, blowing out a massive hole in the base of the popular tourist attraction. The blasts shattered windows far into the Mashona neighborhood and even into the Bluffs, and down the tower fell.

It toppled like a tipped cow at a cow-tipping event. It fell over like a felled redwood, only with no lumberjack nearby to yell "Timber!"

The mighty bull was sent soaring over building tops, finally landing with a tremendous splash into the Aceh Park fountain. Juggling goldfish were launched everywhere.

As Canchim Tower crashed to the ground, Mewati and Lactose Tolerant looked up to see their leader fly overhead, arcing over the top of the moon, which had made an appearance through the dense clouds. Then, with a dual moo, the two took off toward the landing zone. These moos were apparently some sort of cow SOS call, as almost immediately the three nearly rabid calves appeared from the back of the hardware store, launched themselves out through the broken display windows and into the street.

Officer Holstein watched the three younger cows depart, scrambling down the street after their aunts. As they veered left, the officer was sure he could hear a screeching sound.

John, Clarabelle and Officer Holstein stepped outside of the store and almost ran straight into the frightened Ivory Chateaubriand. Startled, Clarabelle shouted out, "Aunt Flossie's corndogs!"

The assistant deputy stopped her mad dash with a rush of relief, safe again, if even for just a short time. The quartet watched as the cows disappeared into the darkness of the Business District, and then turned as a group to look at the rubble from the collapsed tower. About fifty feet off, just in front of the mound of concrete, was the wounded Gail. The bird was about the same size as Lactose Tolerant. The larger Flappy stood next to her and appeared to be licking her bloodied wing.

"I'm fairly certain birds aren't supposed to do that," said Clarabelle.

"I'm fairly certain birds aren't supposed to look like that," countered Officer Holstein.

The Flappus Maximus stopped his licking and looked up, purple eyes glaring directly at the four gawkers. They quickly dashed back into the hardware store.

"What in the hell is going on?" asked a clearly confused Ivory Chateaubriand.

Surprisingly, it was John Steerman who offered up an explanation. "We are in the middle of a war. It's birds versus cows."

"Are you kidding me?" Ivory asked.

"Well, maybe it's cows versus birds," the farmer answered. "It's one of those. And, I have the feeling things are about to get really bad."

"Oh," said Officer Holstein. "I thought they already were."

🐂🐂🐂

Professor Herens had a special affection for Mrs. O'Leary, ever since he took Devon up on the offer to join him, his dad, Caceres and Margaret for a summertime picnic. The two hit it off right away and found they had a lot in common. The woman liked to talk about her goiter and the professor had done a research paper on goiters back when he was a student at AAU. Herens liked discussing anomalies in the English language and Margaret was the only person he knew who kept an animal whose name started with double vowels. The two had laughed and chatted over lemonade and hot dogs on that bright summer afternoon, and, though the professor never told anyone, least of all Margaret O'Leary, about his affections, he thought of that picnic as he helped the slicker-clad woman and her chicken down out of the oak tree. The picnic seemed light-years away from this new kind of hell, the hell of a driving rainstorm, floods and incendiary missiles of poop.

"Are you okay, Margaret?" he asked, once she was lowered gently to the ground.

"How's that?" she asked.

The professor raised his voice. "How are you doing, are you okay?"

Mrs. O'Leary shook her head in acknowledgement. "No worse for the wear, I reckon. I still got all my parts and I managed to find my favorite chicken."

Chicken One seemed quite satisfied to be out of the tree, and was walking around pecking at the grass.

Over the next several minutes, people shared their stories. Margaret described her findings upon making it back into the main part of the farm: lots of stuff knocked about by the first wave, a giant bonfire back behind the barn and the sudden rise of water as the second storm surge came pouring into Contented Corners.

She didn't explain how she found Chicken One or how she made it up the tree to avoid the rush of water, but she did offer up, "I guess I fell asleep up there. I was a might tired."

Devon then explained the dramatic rescue Caceres had executed, pulling him and the professor out of the flooded basement.

"I wondered where you'd headed off to," Margaret said to the farmhand.

"Sí," he said. "That Mr. Steer, he no dummy. Plus, we escape giant python."

Apparently, the Andalusian didn't quite get Devon's explanation about the storm back at the university.

"T'weren't no python," Mrs. O'Leary said. "A giant *tycoon* is headed this way." She emphasized the word as if that would clarify things for Caceres.

Devon and Dr. Herens looked at one another until the professor shrugged his shoulders. There'd be nothing to gain in trying to explain things again.

Then, as though he'd forgotten to get a critical piece of information, Devon asked, "Mrs. O'Leary, do you know where my dad is? Is he okay? We saw the flatbed down on the highway."

"Sí, and Señor Beefy?" added Caceres.

Margaret explained. "It's the cows, Devon. Something horrible has happened. Somehow, they've all changed into... into... something else. Something like cows in a way, but like monsters in another way."

Jaws dropping in unison, the three men were clearly stunned by this turn of events.

Professor Herens asked, "Margaret, do you have any idea what could have made the herd this way?"

Mrs. O'Leary thought the question over for a few seconds and shrugged. "I really don't. I was near certain death in the front of the truck until John pulled me out. I do recall there was a gloppy pile of assorted wood and gunk at the back of the truck that I think was glowing purple for a bit. Then it stopped glowing. Maybe that had something to do with what happened."

The three men looked back down the road and toward the front gate of Contented Corners. None of them had seen a purple gloppy pile on the way in.

Mrs. O'Leary continued. "They headed up the highway, toward Lineback Street. Your dad headed off after them, Devon."

After that, it didn't take much discussion for the group to decide they'd best get to finding John and the mutated herd. Caceres decided to stay at the farm. He needed to make sure the fires were put out. Plus he didn't want to lose any more of his prized flowers. Most of the ones that were used in the landscaping had been washed away, but there was a greenhouse off behind the toolshed.

The professor got behind the wheel of the pickup and Margaret scooched in between him and Devon, her chicken sitting safely on her lap. Herens looked in his side mirror and saw the faithful Caceres waving his goodbye to them all. Before they left, the gardener had told the trio he'd protect the plants and the farm come hell or high water, a phrase he'd heard on television. And with the dozens of fires still blazing and another storm surge no doubt on the way, Herens just had to chuckle.

Though the flower enthusiast most likely didn't realize it, he had just laid down prophecy. Hell and high water indeed.

The good news just kept coming in. The aliens' successful scan of the Centralized Valley had led to similar scans of regions all over the planet.

"This 'Earth,' as it is called, will be perfect for the relocation of our people," Crewmember Two predicted. "And this area over the Southern Hemisphere, this would-be rain forest with the gigantic river, is being transformed at a pace I wouldn't have believed possible."

"Indeed," said Crewmember One. "My calculations tell me these beings are transforming more than sixty thousand acres a day of unusable forests into prime grazing land. It is phenomenal."

Both crewmembers mooed in delight.

Crewmember One continued, "And, you may not believe this, but my scans are showing signs of intelligent life."

"What?" asked Crewmember Two in surprise. "How can that be?"

"I am not certain," replied the alien cow. "There was nothing in the preliminary scans other than the fact that there is life here, and a bit of it looks like us."

"Go on," said his traveling companion.

"Well, one of those creatures who looks like us apparently thinks like us too. I guess they are not all gum-chewing morons."

"Where is this superior-thinking creature? Tell me," said the other crewmember.

"That's the crazy thing," said Crewmember One. "The scan shows this being is up on the peninsula next to that large valley to the north we previously surveyed."

"But we've already been there. The scan showed nothing earlier," said Crewmember Two.

"Yet here it is, see for yourself."

Crewmember One held up the portable scanner screen. Sure enough, a bright blue-grey dot was blinking rapidly right over the top of Bay City.

"Isn't that the location of the giant industrial complex we saw in the distance during our survey?" asked the curious cow traveler.

"I believe the term here is 'city.' I think that is a city," the other answered.

"'City?' That is quite a funny term," opined the bovine.

The duo mooed in laughter for several seconds.

"'City,' how ridiculous," one of them said.

After they'd regrouped, Crewmember Two offered an observation. "It might be tough to find the superior being in amongst the industrial area and in the midst of many inferior beings."

"That it might," said Crewmember One. "What do you suggest?"

"Find some sort of building, a landmark even. Look for one with a large open space next to it and launch the homing beacon to that location. It will draw the superior being to the area, and we can head there and see what this is all about."

"Okay, but don't you think that's dangerous? We don't know what the beings here are capable of, other than the rapid transformation of land regions."

Crewmember Two considered the risks for a few moments, and then mooed in laughter, patting his companion on the back with his hoof. "How dangerous can they be? They call their industrial complexes 'city.'"

The raucous moo laughter could be heard throughout the ship.

🐂🐂🐂

Typhoon Bessie continued to hammer down upon Bay City. The erratic winds uprooted ancient, huge trees throughout the peninsula and cut off power to many thousands of homes. The rain drove down in pelting sheets, changing directions with impossible randomness, flooding out neighborhoods and terrifying raccoons.

Band after band of the freak storm swept over the region, and the sea surged inland, wiping away beloved sea-level monuments like the Limia Nagori Big Toe Statue and the Schwyz Toothpick Memorial Outhouse.

Up on Lineback Street, the Flappus Maximus was oblivious to the cataclysm, so focused was he on his beloved mate. Mutated seagull spit, it appears, has amazing healing capabilities. The ability to lick, as well as the addition of an unusual opposable tongue, was a bonus effect of the excessive radiation that Flappy didn't know he had. The enormous gull only knew that Gail was hurt and hoped he could help.

And help he did. The restorative capabilities of the mucous-like substance had the Gull Primus up and flying around in no time, and shortly thereafter Flappy called a strategizing session, addressing the quartet of smaller gulls.

FLEDGLINGS! GOOFBALL, SNAP, LOUIE, MOE. WE HAVE NO TIME TO MOURN THE VAPORIZATION OF YOUR BROTHERS. PEABRAIN AND KNUCKLEHEAD GAVE THEIR LIVES FOR THE FLOCK. NOW WE MUST ENGAGE THE VILE BEASTS. GATHER 'ROUND. I SHALL LAY OUT OUR CLEVER YET EFFECTIVE STRATEGY. MAKE NO MISTAKE. THESE COWS ARE TOAST.

The mutated gulls closed ranks and formed a circle around their leader. Within a half an hour after Canchim Tower fell, the birds lined up in a row across Lineback Street, like a warped posse from the Old West, and hopped their way north toward where Beefy had crash-landed.

Down at the Aceh Park fountain, a similar scene unfolded. The cows expressed relief (as if such an emotion was possible to express through a common moo) at the fact that Beefy was unharmed after his two-hundred-yard flight. Landing in the fountain had been fortuitous indeed, and served as the impetus to get the animals together as a cohesive group. The head of the herd mooed out instructions, indicating that things were quite serious.

FEAR NOT, MY HERD. I AM UNHARMED. YET, DESPITE THAT FACT, OUR SITUATION IS DIRE. THE SUDDEN APPEARANCE OF THE HUMAN FARMER AND MY FLIGHT FROM THE TOWER HAVE REVEALED TO ME THE TRUTH OF THINGS. THE HUMANS ARE NOT

*THE ENEMY. THE HUMANS ARE SIMPLY WITHOUT
CLUE. IT'S THE BIRDS. THE BIRDS ARE EVIL. THEY
MUST BE DESTROYED.*

*NOW, COME IN CLOSE – YES, YOU TOO, LITTLE
ONES – AND I SHALL REVEAL TO YOU OUR BATTLE
PLAN.*

Huey, Curly and Crackle calmed down a significant degree
and smiled with their pointy teeth, listening to the plan that
Beefy was laying out. Mewati and Lactose Tolerant confidently shook their heads in unison, mooing their buy-in to
the strategy. Even the previously erratic Kenana was present
and accounted for, all remnants of prior panic gone from the
huge beast. This was a good thing, Beefy reasoned, as the
super-sized cow would play an important part in what the
bull knew was coming: the showdown with the seagulls.

And so, as if they were a mirror image of the flying mutants
just down the road, the Contented Corners creatures also
spread out across Lineback Street, facing the destroyed tower.
And, amidst typhoon rains and whipping wind, they began to
walk slowly south, with Beefy mooing out each step, like a
deformed drill sergeant. One moo, one step. Moo. Moo. Moo.
Moo. The herd marched ahead.

Shortly after the row of birds hopped past the brightly lit Hays
Converter Hardware and on down the road, John Steerman's
pickup pulled into a parking spot directly in front of the store.
Within a few seconds, Mrs. O'Leary, Devon and Professor
Herens rushed in. It was with great relief they immediately
laid eyes on the dairy farmer, who was standing in a circle
with a police officer and a couple of ladies. They appeared
to be looking at a sawed-off shotgun one of the women was
holding.

"Dad!" Devon yelled. He rushed up and gave his father a
big hug.

John patted his son on the shoulder, offering up a sort
of half embrace. He wasn't too comfortable with physical
contact. He tipped his invisible hat. "Son," he said.

The next several minutes were spent with introductions and copious amounts of bowing and hat tipping, "Ma'ams" and "Can't complains," and explanations of the current state of events and everyone's adventures up to that point. Mrs. O'Leary, holding on tightly to her chicken, had to have several things said twice owing to her poor hearing. This included finally getting the tycoon/typhoon misunderstanding sorted out. In the end, everyone seemed at least partially clear on what had transpired.

After Devon handed his dad the whittled yeti he'd grabbed from the farmhouse, he said, "There's something I don't quite understand. I get the typhoon and the cow mutations. But what I don't get is the birds. We saw them hopping down the street as we were driving around the tower rubble. They seem as mutated as the cattle you described. Where in the world did they come from?"

"I think I can help here," offered Officer Holstein. "Before the storm, Assistant Deputy Chateaubriand – who was still citizen Ivory Chateaubriand at the time – and I were up on the observation platform of Canchim Tower. This was before the tower fell over."

The policeman paused to ensure everyone was following his story so far. They appeared to be. Even Chicken One was looking, rapt, at the polite man.

He continued, "Well I was called to that location to investigate a mysterious object floating offshore." He paused again. Everyone was still with him. He went on. "Though it was impossible to make a positive identification, I reasoned it was most likely that what we were looking at was some sort of sea serpent, and for some reason it seemed to me it had bad intent. I reported the sighting to headquarters in quick fashion."

"But what does that have to do with what appear to be dynamically mutated sea birds?" Devon asked.

For the second time in the last several hours, Officer Holstein internally chastised himself for his own poor performance. He thought his description of events would ensure the complete understanding of all, but clearly he'd failed in that endeavor. Self-doubt began to settle in the mind of the policeman. He stopped mid-story, searching his brain for the right words.

Ivory Chateaubriand continued the explanation. "Whether that floating object was a sea serpent or something far more insidious, two things were immediately apparent to both of us. First, it was purple. No doubt about it. Believe me, I know purple. It wasn't violet or mauve or anything like that. It was purple; the exact same purple as an eggplant. And the exact same color as the eyes of those cows..."

"What was the other thing?" asked Professor Herens, who'd been formulating his own idea regarding the origin of the mutated herd.

Ivory concluded, "Well, the other thing was that, above the floating thing, up in the sky just circling around, were a bunch of seagulls. Of that I'm certain."

Officer Holstein nodded his agreement. Ivory was spot on.

Dr. Herens then spoke up. "Well, I think that seals it."

Margaret O'Leary, who had heard about half of what had just been said, interrupted. "Oh, great, so now we've got seal monsters too?"

Chicken One clucked in derision.

"No, no," Herens continued. "This floating purple object must have been the source of immense radiation. It most likely mutated the birds that landed on it into flying freaks of nature and then did the same to the dear farm animals. It was probably carried ashore by the typhoon storm surge. When that surge tipped over the flatbed, the herd was probably mutated by that same floating purple radiation pile."

John Steerman listened intently to all the explanations that were going on. He didn't say anything, just gripped and twisted his yeti in his clenched right hand. His eyes grew dark, his brow furrowed. The farmer was not happy. This was getting personal. These were his cows.

It was Devon who spoke next, uttering what most everyone in the group was now thinking.

He said, with great confidence, "Holy Cow!"

ᘓᕊᘓᕊᘓᕊ

As soon as the Flappus Maximus caught sight of the row of cattle, he screeched out his signal to attack. Intent upon separating the herd, he and the Gull Primus lifted in flight, into the driving rain, to launch attacks from the east and the west, coming in low over the building tops, zig-zag-ging between lightning strikes and crashing into the closest bovine. The smaller birds, Goofball, Snap, Louie and Moe, swooped and swirled around the herd in all directions like so many pesky gnats; vulture-sized gnats with purple eyes and eagle talons.

Beefy's plan had been for the line of cows to fall back and form a circle behind the massive Kenana once the fighting began, but the herd mentality didn't quite take effect. The idea was to defend and attack, a sort of block and jab approach. The group got in proper circular alignment once the birds lifted into the sky. However, as Beefy dropped low to begin a terror-moo, his telepathic instructions ceased and the rest of the beasts just scattered. Kenana wandered off toward the muumuu shop, Lactose Tolerant headed straight for the leather store and Mewati ran around in circles, acting confused. As for the little ones, Curly took a few sniffs of the air and tore off down Lineback Street, his siblings giving chase. In short order they crashed into the Chicken Coop restaurant and began devouring all of the meat they could find.

Beefy was about halfway through the terror-moo buildup, when he was knocked out of the moo and tipped over by a direct hit from the Flappus Maximus. The bull landed on his side with a thud, up to his tail in standing water. Flappy hopped toward the beast, swiping with his left talon. The bull started flailing his legs, and his hoof horns proved to be quite effective, jabbing into the bird on several occasions.

The Gull Primus slammed headfirst into the side of Kenana and went sprawling, knocked a bit loopy. Mewati was on her in an instant, blasting the bird with dragon fire. Gail lifted a wing for protection and that seemed to do the trick. The bird's feathers were completely fireproof. That didn't stop the dragon-cow however, as she let out a continuous onslaught of intense flame as long as her breath held out.

Meanwhile, Lactose Tolerant glared into the Galloway House of Leather. The mutated cow was able to hate, and she hated the place with a passion. She put her attempts at destroying the gull creatures on hold, aligned herself with the front of the building and started spraying out of her right udder. The acid dissolved most substances it came in contact with, and, in under a minute, the front display area and entryway were completely gone. With that development, the cow walked into the center of the store and let loose with a double-barrel attack that turned the place into a Hazmat nightmare. The cowhide emporium virtually melted away.

Back at the battle, the four smaller, yet still quite impressively large birds, dove straight into Kenana with little effect. Goofball slammed directly on top of the cow's back and immediately was held fast by the re-activated adhesion field that had previously held Officer Holstein. The bird let out a series of screeches and squawks to warn the others to stay away from the elephant-cow's back.

At that, Flappy let out a loud, instructional caw and off the flock flew, sans Goofball, to regroup and attack again. Beefy was back on his feet in no time, mooing the others to his side for a reassessment of their own. The three calves did not heed Beefy's moo, so engrossed were they in their newfound feast. Beefy reconsidered his options, understanding that he'd need to start his terror-moo much earlier if it was to have an impact on the battle. The bull still had his death-spin in his arsenal and, who knows, maybe there were other mutations within in the group that had yet to be brought to light.

And so, into the night and through the storm the battle raged. Wave after wave of bird attacks, some successful, some not so much. The war was on, and the war was fierce.

🐃 🐃 🐃

Most everyone in the RV had fallen asleep. Siri Batangas, donning headphones so as not to disturb his exhausted companions, and so he could hear the television over the slamming rain, was watching the fourth movie in the Shirley Tempkin marathon that was being broadcast on Channel Five. No other local channel was on the air, it appeared. The marathon had launched with yet another showing of the classic *Hidee*, and at first the group in the DBP had kept the channel on in case meteorologist Bo Vine broke in with a local weather report, or some other update on the storm.

But there was no coverage of the storm to be seen on either the local or national news channels, or even the weather channels, since they were all off the air.

"This is not good," Brad the cow mascot, also still awake, had offered up, concentrating on his smartphone, which would not connect to the Internet.

Batangas answered in his still-developing mimicry of the old-time child actress. "Why is that, grandfather?" he asked.

The impression was getting better. It was quite amazing.

The cow mascot, still in full outfit (sans head), replied, "Well, I have lived in earthquake country for my entire life, and I have been in a few big ones. If you are in the middle of a big city during a major earthquake and want to know where the epicenter is, look for the place where there are no reports of damage, the place where no word of any kind is getting out. That is usually the worst-hit location."

Batangas stood up and curtsied. "I see, grandfather. And there is no information about the tornado or the hail or anything, right?"

Brad was amazed by the thoroughness of this man's dedication to his craft. He could only aspire to be such a pretend cow.

"Correct," he replied. "Since there are no news reports of any kind from here, no fire engine sirens or police action, it's safe to say that tornadoes or hail are hitting the whole region. Or maybe even worse. Who knows what's happening out there. A lot of people are dead because of all this, I can assure you. This is not good at all."

"Oh my," Siri responded. He furrowed his brow, but still tried to look cute, just like the famous tot.

In his mind, things could be worse. Everyone in the RV was safe. The Henchman had made some fantastic tea and they had Cookies Galore (the snack, not the famous exotic dancer) in abundance. When Dutch had brought them out on a fancy tray, Batangas had thrown back his head with joy, diving into his old-time European movie star accent.

"Biscuits!" he'd exclaimed. "Jolly good. Jolly good indeed."

This had made everyone laugh, except for the bullfighter, who was still swishing away in the back of the room.

Apparently, the airing of the movie marathon was some sort of preprogrammed default autopilot for when Channel

Five was knocked offline. Siri privately was thrilled to have the opportunity to study the child actress, uninterrupted, for an extended period of time. Besides, he reasoned, any news reports that did come on would most likely not provide any actual help, but would add to the overall stress of the situation. So, despite the raging storm, things were about as good as they could get, for now.

Just a couple of hours before sunrise, as the famous entertainer was pantomiming along to Shirley Tempkin's signature song, "Hopping from Cow to Cow" from the classic film *The Wacky West*, a sudden loud, metallic, grinding and crashing sound blasted through the RV.

All the previously sleeping occupants of the DBP were awake in an instant, Red calling out, "What in tarnation?"

Bright, multi-colored flashing lights could now be seen through the RV's window. The metallic grinding noise increased and then stopped.

Within a minute, the men, other than Siri, who was absorbed in his movie, headed for the door. For a second, Dutch considered offering to stay behind to get some fresh tea brewing, but thought better of it and brought up the rear as the group went down the steps and out into the rain once again.

Batangas sat, watching the movie and singing along quietly, "I hop to you, I hop to you, moo diddle moo diddle moo moo moo."

The sight outside was astonishing. At least they all knew where the metallic sound had come from. A few of the mangled trucks, the ones closest by, were clearly visible in the bright light given off from the RV. One extra-long Tauros, a raised front, three-wheel drive super longbed model, with windows smashed out from the grapefruit-sized hail, had been pierced. Not like an ear or nose piercing, but rather pierced like being pierced with a spear. Except this was no spear.

Protruding upward through the center of the super longbed portion of the rig was a cylindrical metallic object, twenty feet tall and four feet in diameter. It was the source of the flashing colored lights; they were all over the thing. The grinding noise had come from the object ripping through the truck bed and into the ground below. The cylinder must have been the base of the object because there was a tall, skinny pole that stretched out of it another ten feet upward. The pole moved up and down, extending away from and descending into the base section. And, there was another light, star-shaped, at the top of the pole that flashed in what appeared to be a coded pattern.

"It looks like a Christmas tree," offered up Brad.

Red nodded and said, "Yeah, if the Christmas tree was three times taller than your house, was made of metal and looked like the world's largest butter churn."

"Houston, we have a problem," said Brad.

Back and forth the battle raged on toward sunrise. The wind and the rain slammed Lineback Street but seemed to have no effect on the combatants. The humans watched from a safe distance, waiting for things to play out. At times they'd huddle under a windswept awning, or dash into the relative safety of one of the stores. As the mutated creatures slowly destroyed their way toward the north end of the street and the top of the switchbacks, their audience went with them.

After a while, the terror of it all began to seem normal. Professor Herens and Margaret O'Leary launched into discussions about goiters and the alphabet, picking up where'd they'd left off so long ago back at Contented Corners. John even sat down, right out in the weather, on a bench at Aceh Park, just feet from the fountain where Beefy had crash-landed. He took out his pocketknife and set to whittling, fine-tuning his tiny yeti. Only on occasion would Clarabelle let loose with one of her custom expletives. She carried the store's sawed-off shotgun at her side, even though, when they'd inspected it, they'd discovered the thing wasn't loaded.

None of this is to imply that the humans in any way had become complacent, or that the battle was boring. That wasn't the case. It's just that the mooing, screeching, scratching and death-spins came to be, in the viewpoint of the seven observers, less traumatic than at first. It was the intermittent explosions that kept the group alert. Kenana had perfected the dropping and detonating of the steaming C-4 pies, and had leveled the Offal House with two seemingly calculated and strategically placed mounds of explosives.

"Maple-carpeted tractor!" screamed Clarabelle, startled by the sudden blasts. A few minutes later, as the chilly wind whipped up again and the fighting intensified across the street, the hardware store night manager exclaimed, "I'd give my right toe for a cup of coffee right now."

A see-saw of emotion, a dichotomy of terror and familiarity, had settled over the septet.

⌐⌐⌐⌐⌐⌐

The battle had progressed up Lineback and had reached a spot adjacent to the twin fast food restaurants, the Burger Joint and the Chicken Coop. When Beefy saw Crackle, Curly and Huey inside the chicken restaurant, he mooed stern orders for the three calves to rejoin the herd. Snarling their disapproval, the calves dashed back out into the street, the obstinate Crackle still munching on several chicken wings.

But then, the hefty leader caught sight of the restaurant next door, the Burger Joint, and was outraged, rearing up on his back legs and letting out a ferocious yell. In an instant, the fighting stopped.

Beefy's cry was followed immediately by the dual screams of Flappy and Gail, who had just realized the nature of the business that was conducted at the Chicken Coop. The Gull Primus charged, hopping and jumping toward the six-foot fiberglass chicken that had been positioned near the front door of the restaurant. She leapt up, grabbing the chicken's head in her giant talons. Beating her massive wings powerfully, she tore the statue out of its concrete base and flew high up into the air, carrying the statue toward the ocean. Cattle and gulls watched Gail soar westward, giant chicken in her grasp, silhouetted by the lightning-filled sky.

Once the Gull Primus disappeared from view into the storm and over the rooftops of Berrenda Bluffs, Beefy and Flappy looked intensely at one another. They both nodded, as if to say there were currently bigger fish to fry, and turned their attention toward the more immediate threat: fast food.

The maddened bull charged, his massive horns obliterating the doorway to the burger establishment. The rest of the herd, save for the freshly distracted trio of little ones, raged into the building and issued forth an incredible array of mutated cow destruction. Upon entry, Kenana, Goofball still held fast to her back, began dropping pie explosives with a regularity hinting at a prune-filled diet. Lactose Tolerant, now masterful at aiming her acid shots, attacked the kitchen equipment. The deli cooler and the combo thermal oven and fryers dissolved in an instant into a green ooze, stainless steel evaporating like teardrops on the surface of the sun. Mewati let loose with dragon fire, torching the restaurant ceiling before moving on to incinerate the seating area, soda machine and the dumpster located just outside the back door. As for Beefy, he launched into a series of death-spins, smashing through walls and collapsing the structure. Within a minute, the Burger Joint lay in a mangled mess of fiery, acidy goo.

Next door, the Chicken Coop collapsed, a victim of Flappy's vicious jackhammer beak and chainsaw-like talons. The smaller birds did the best they could to assist. Snap ripped at the gas ovens while Louie made quick work of the janitor's closet and Moe managed to upend the cash registers, sending currency of every type flying in all directions. Once the structure started to give way, the massive Flappus Maximus spread his wings wide to protect the smaller birds, effectively shielding them from the cascading rafters.

Moments later, both farm animals and sea birds stood together and watched the ruins burn. Gail, back from depositing the giant chicken somewhere less dangerous, flew down to join Flappy. Flappy wrapped a wing around his mate, pulling her close, just as Kenana's cow pies detonated in rapid succession. BOOM BOOM BOOM BOOM. Shortly after, the pile of rubble that had been the Chicken Coop exploded in a massive blast, gas from the shredded oven lines igniting in a fire ball that shot a hundred feet up into the stormy sky. The blast rocked the entire boulevard, inspiring a raucous round of moos and shrieks from the animal observers.

After a couple more moments of contemplation, Beefy and Flappy once again made eye contact. They nodded at one another and, with a screech, Flappy took off south, flying back down Lineback Street toward the ruined tower. Gail, Moe, Louie and Snap followed in flight. Goofball squawked, flailing wildly on Kenana's back.

Beefy addressed the three cows.

> *THIS IS NOT OVER. THE ENEMY IS REGROUPING.*
> *THE ENEMY WILL RETURN. MEWATI, LACTOSE*
> *TOLERANT, YOU ARE TO FIND THE LITTLE ONES.*
> *BRING THEM TO US. KENANA, YOU ARE TO COME*
> *WITH ME. THERE IS SOMETHING I MUST DO.*

North of the Burger Joint was Officer Holstein's favorite store, A China Shop. Beefy had noticed the store as he watched the conflagration minutes earlier, and felt drawn to it. He knew he had to get inside. He knew it was a holy place. The bull addressed Kenana.

> *YOU ARE TO GUARD THE ENTRY. ALLOW NO ONE*
> *INSIDE.*

The massive Kenana stood in protection of the place. Beefy lightly stepped in and looked around. Careful to make sure his massive horns didn't damage a single piece, the giant bull seemed to relax in the place. His hide sagged a bit and he let out a sighing, gentle moo. A serene sense of ease enveloped the head of the herd. After all the chaos of the past several hours, the influx of peace settled the beast's previously rattled senses. All anger left. Any fear dissipated. Only calmness remained, a calmness that came with a memory. A peaceful tune Beefy had learned as a calf. A tranquil hymn from his youth. It resonated through the bull's every fiber, like a wave of cotton candy.

> *OHM--*
> *OHM—*
> *OH, M'DARLIN', OH M'DARLIN', OH M'DARLIN',*
> *CLEMENTINE...*

Beefy was at peace.

From their new location across the street at the Moore Cowbell music store, the seven humans could see right into A China Shop. Officer Holstein also sagged and sighed, clearly relieved that his favorite store would not be damaged, and clearly confused by the fact the place seemed chock-full of dishware.

Ivory offered up an opinion. "Well that's something you hear a lot about but never see. It's a darn bull in a china shop."

"Literally," added the observant Devon.

But there wasn't much time for such sublimity, for within seconds the gulls were back on the street and within minutes the battle had resumed. Eventually the fighting advanced north to the end of the Business District and the top of the switchbacks, and Beefy changed course, moving west down the last available intersecting road, Braford Street. The birds followed along.

"What are they doing?" asked a worried Ivory. "My house is down that street!"

There were several shrugs at first, but then Dr. Herens spoke up. "I think I know, miss."

"I haven't been called 'miss' since I was sixteen," snapped Ivory. She was clearly concerned about these latest developments.

The professor responded. "I'm sorry, ma'am. I've been watching this battle. I think I know what's going on and I don't think your home is in any danger of a direct attack."

Devon chimed in. "Tell us, Professor, what do you think is happening?"

The professor answered. "It seems to me that Beefy knows exactly what he is doing. For the most part, unless a sudden situational change requires immediate action, the bull is leading the birds to a specific destination."

"Where would that be, Dr. Herens?" asked Officer Holstein.

"He's leading them to the Rock House Restaurant. You know, the steak house that hangs out over the rocks? Unless I miss my guess, the bull has something in mind that requires moving the fight to that location."

"You don't think that..." began Clarabelle.

"I do indeed," Herens completed the night manager's sentence for her. "The cows and birds are headed for a final showdown. It'll be the herd versus the flock. Cow-o e gull-o."

"Frog-laden coupons," replied Clarabelle, almost to herself.

⚞⚟ ⚞⚟ ⚞⚟

It turns out cows really can climb stairs, and, if they need to, a lot of them.

After several hours of tubular, mondo wave-riding, Aliab, Dingo and their new friend, Mrs. Beefy, were exhausted. Dingo had taken the muumuu from her longboard and tied it around the mid-section of the cow, to the absolute delight of Aliab. None of the dozens of other surfers who had decided to brave the enormous waves seemed to notice that there was a cow riding a door in their midst. Either that, or they didn't care. Surfers are typically unconventional, and the surfing community at the Bluffs was a typical surfing community. For certain the unconventional group had seen a lot of unconventional things, and a surfing cow probably just wasn't something to get too worked up about.

The veteran boarder Aliab knew the danger of surfing when tired, or hungry for that matter, and after a particularly gnarly ride he gave Dingo the appropriate hand signals that meant, "I'm tired – time to go." The roommates had their own hand signal language specifically to be used when surfing, and if either of them gave the signal to go, both of them would climb the staircase and head back to their tiny house without hesitation. But, when Aliab and Dingo headed for the stairs this time, Mrs. Beefy followed along, her door amazingly balanced across her back.

"Dude," Aliab said, "the cow's following us. She must be exhausted too."

Dingo opened the sliding glass doors that faced the perimeter deck and the ocean beyond, and Mrs. Beefy walked right in. Tossing the metal door onto the couch, the novice surfing cow lay down and fell fast asleep, right there in the living room.

Dingo saw the cow's eyes close and said, laughing, "Dude, I was gonna offer her some pizza. Well, more for us, huh?"

Aliab wasn't paying attention. He'd received several messages on his phone, and some texts to boot. All of the messages were from Piney Woods, the surfing legend Dingo had called to report the possible Marinhoa.

"What's that, brah?" he said.

"Dude, we have a cow in our living room." Dingo was quite amazed.

Aliab started dialing his phone. "It's Piney Woods, he called like a million times."

Dingo diverted her attention from the sleeping cow to the matter at hand. She could only hear her roommate's side of the conversation.

"Dude. ... What? ... Dude. ... Okay. ... Bye, dude."

And with that, the surfer clicked his phone off. He took a large swig of an orange soda.

"Brah, what is up?" asked a now-curious Dingo.

"I guess the waves are nothing to mess around with. Piney says it's all over the news over in Australia. Brah, we're in the middle of a typhoon."

"No way!" said Dingo.

"Way," replied Aliab. "I wonder if everyone's okay. Piney said it's real bad."

The surfers had no clue about the collapse of Canchim Tower or the mayhem on Lineback Street. Dingo took a look out the kitchen window. It faced east, away from the ocean and out toward Mashona Town. The sky was lit up.

"Dude, I think there are some buildings on fire over by Lineback," said Dingo.

Aliab grabbed a piece of pizza and headed over to see for himself. The two of them stood side by side for several minutes trying to gauge the severity of the situation.

"Brah, it's pouring outside. How is that even possible?" Aliab asked.

Dingo yawned. "I'm beat. I need to lie down for a while."

Aliab nodded his agreement. "Me too, brah," he said. "It'll be light soon. Let's catch thirty winks and get back down to the water. The waves should still be awesome."

"Should be," agreed Dingo, stretching out in a recliner.

Aliab flipped off the lights and flopped down on the couch. The pair was asleep within a couple of minutes.

In the center of the room, Mrs. Beefy began to snore.

About ninety restful minutes later, the cow mooed. Dingo sprang out of the chair and dashed into the kitchen. She'd taken to wearing her wetsuit practically all of the time in emulation of her mentor, and its neoprene squeaked as she headed over. The squeaking, rather than the mooing, woke the amiable Aliab.

"Brah, what are you doing?" he asked, rubbing the sleep out of his eyes.

"Dude, our cow is hungry. She's all mooing and stuff."

Dingo opened the refrigerator. There was pizza and orange soda inside. The lady surfer opened the vegetable crisper just in case something might be there. The drawer had never been opened before.

"What are you looking for, brah?" Aliab asked. "We probably have what we always have in there. Unless somebody stocked it for us again. There's cereal in the cupboard. Maybe the cow likes Chocolatoos right out of the box like we do. They are righteous."

Dingo continued to slide pizza boxes around in the fridge. "Do we have any cud?"

"Any what?" her roommate asked.

"Cud, like in, 'cows chew cud.' I guess that's what they eat." Dingo closed the appliance door.

Mrs. Beefy let out another moo.

"Do you know if they sell cud down at the market?" she asked.

Somewhere back in her mind it seemed to Dingo like she should know this stuff. Becoming a surfer had caused her to forget a lot of things she used to know.

"Dang, if only the cow was laughing, I'd know what to feed her," offered up Aliab.

"What would that be, dude?" Dingo asked.

Aliab smiled and answered, "Cheese, brah. Everyone knows you feed a laughing cow cheese."

The two surfers cracked up in delight. Mrs. Beefy appeared to smile.

Aliab stood up and grabbed his board. "Oh, well, probably we'll have to order it online, brah, once we get some moolah."

The pair burst out laughing again.

Aliab continued. "I wonder if she'll eat seaweed. Anyway, I'm heading back down. It's light out."

"Not without me and the cow, you're not, dude. Besides, she's probably all worked up because she needs to get back up on her door."

And, thinking that she probably should know whether or not cows eat seaweed, Dingo guided Mrs. Beefy out through the sliding glass door and onto the deck.

A sudden question popped into her mind and she said to the cow, "What's your name, cow? I've got to give you a name."

Dingo struggled a bit, but managed to set the large surfing door on top of the cow. Mrs. Beefy mooed again, and stomped her hooves in excitement.

"Wow, you really do love to surf," Dingo said. "Let's get down to the waves, cow."

Aliab was already halfway down the stairs.

ᘉ ᘉ ᘉ

Beefy was not omniscient.

Professor Herens was partially correct when he intimated that the bull was super-intelligent. He was, as far as bulls go. The mutation he'd gone through had made him a self-aware creature, like a human. He could communicate with his herd (though they had a tough time following orders), he was aware of his environment and he had some sense of purpose. And he could, to a limited degree, create a plan and act on it, which, in the realm of cowdom, was quite an accomplishment. There were probably only two other bovine-looking creatures in the vicinity of Earth that could do that, and they were both in a spaceship.

But there was no way Beefy could have known that a large steakhouse, positioned high above huge, jagged boulders and a roiling sea, was just down the street when he turned left off Lineback and into the Mashona neighborhood. Had he continued north, the street would have dipped down into a series of seventeen tight and twisty turns as it dropped down to the popular Fishyman's Wharf, but Beefy didn't notice this and, in his mind, making a left was the only option.

So, off the herd went and, for a while, caught a respite from the relentless gulls. A few hundred feet down the road, northeast of the intersection of Braford and Criollo Streets, Beefy and the cows came to a large parking lot and the Rock House Restaurant. He sent Mewati and Lactose Tolerant to the left and right of the building to conduct a quick site survey.

He instructed Kenana to break down the entry doors to the restaurant and he and the gigantic beast stepped inside. Kenana barely fit under the doorway.

The view from almost all points of the restaurant, including the foyer, was stunning. The whole expanse of the spectacular Big Bridge, all lit up in the predawn darkness, was something Beefy could appreciate. He offered up a quick moo in C-minor, the bovine equivalent of "Wow!"

It didn't take long for the smart bull to conceive a plan, and soon the two cow scouts had returned and all four of the beasts were standing near the restaurant host station. The reconnaissance mission had revealed a single path leading around the west side of the structure to the back of the establishment where there was a massive wooden deck that jutted out over the crashing waves where patrons could eat outside whenever the weather allowed. (The current weather didn't allow.)

Beefy's plan was simple. It had to be, there was only so much the cows could understand. He gathered the trio and mooed out his instructions.

> *WE SHALL END THIS BATTLE HERE, MY HERD.*
> *AND WE SHALL PREVAIL. I SHALL MOCK THE BIRDS,*
> *INSULT THEIR LOOKS AND THEIR HERITAGE, AND*
> *CHALLENGE THEM TO COME INTO THE BUILDING.*

He looked directly at Lactose Tolerant and continued mooing.

> *YOU ARE TO POSITION YOURSELF ON THE SIDE OF*
> *THE BUILDING, RIGHT NEXT TO THE ENTRY TO THE*
> *PLATFORM.*

Beefy nodded toward the suspended deck behind the Rock House. He went on.

> *ONCE KENANA AND I RUN PAST YOU, RAIN ACID*
> *DOWN UPON THE PLATFORM. DO YOU UNDERSTAND?*

Lactose Tolerant nodded and mooed. Beefy continued, fixing his gaze on the dragon-cow.

MEWATI. HIDE YOURSELF, OVER THERE. TRY TO BLEND IN TO YOUR SURROUNDINGS.

Beefy motioned a few feet away, at the restrooms.

ON MY SIGNAL, YOU ARE TO RUN OUTSIDE AND THEN LIGHT UP THIS ENTRYWAY. BURN EVERYTHING. IS THAT CLEAR?

Mewati snorted her understanding, small flames shooting from her snout. Beefy turned to face Kenana. Goofball, still stuck to her back, let out a series of helpless squawks.

NOW KENANA, YOU ARE TO PLACE EXPLOSIVES THROUGHOUT THE STRUCTURE. THEN YOU AND I WILL HEAD OUT THE BACK DOORS. WE SHALL ESCAPE TO SAFETY WITH LACTOSE TOLERANT. THE ENEMY WILL BE TRAPPED. THE BUILDING WILL EXPLODE. DO YOU FOLLOW?

The massive cow nodded her huge head, signaling her understanding.

I SHALL DESTROY THE INSIDES OF THIS PLACE TO SLOW THE ENEMY. I WILL GUIDE AND DIRECT YOU, MY HERD. NOW, GO. MEWATI, HIDE AS BEST YOU CAN. LACTOSE TOLERANT, GO THROUGH THE BACK AND GET IN POSITION JUST OFF THE PLATFORM. KENANA, IT IS TIME FOR PIES. GO... NOW.

Beefy turned and stepped through what had been the front doors of the Rock House before Kenana had burst in. The entryway was a shattered mess of wood and doorknobs.

The herd was ready, ready to end the fight with the gulls, once and for all.

⧪⧪⧪

Once the cows turned off Lineback Street and headed west under the trees, the Flappus Maximus directed his flock to fly, and as one they lifted up above the foliage-draped street. The wind-whipped trees along this section of Braford Street were old and massive, forming a complete canopy over the roadway. The wind and rain had subsided and now a light mist fell upon the residential neighborhood.

Flappy was born with exceptional vision, even for a far-sighted seagull. The mutation had only made this sense more acute. He could now register the heat signature of the running animals as they rumbled along under the cover of the huge trees. The bird leader guessed that the cows had lowered their guard, figuring they were invisible from the air under the dense cover. He gave a caw of delight, and let the flock in on his little secret.

THE BEASTS THINK THEY ARE SAFE. THEY THINK THEY CANNOT BE SEEN. BUT I AM THE FLAPPUS MAXIMUS. I SEE ALL. I SEE THE LITTLE ONES. THEY'VE ABANDONED THE REST OF THE GROUP. CAW, MY FLOCK. CAW IN DERISION AT THE STUPIDITY OF THESE CREATURES.

It was true. Flappy could see the three little cows peel off from the rest of the herd, leaping as a group headlong into a large construction dumpster parked in front of a home that was being remodeled. Though Gail couldn't see what was so clear to her leader, she cawed nonetheless, loyal to her mate. As they continued to fly above the herd, all the birds cawed, a derisive, critical caw of disdain.

And once Beefy stopped the cows in front of the restaurant, Flappy called out instructions to the others.

TO ME, IN CLOSE, MY FLOCK. WE HAVE THEM NOW.

The gulls flew in close and, as a group, the birds hovered above the restaurant parking lot.

THE BEASTS HAVE ENSURED THEIR OWN DEFEAT. THERE IS NO DOUBT THEY WILL ENTER THE STRUCTURE BELOW. THERE IS NO DOUBT THAT, ONCE THEY DO SO, THEY WILL BE TRAPPED. AND LASTLY,

THERE IS NO DOUBT THAT OUR SUPERIOR STRENGTH,
AGILITY AND INTELLIGENCE WILL WIN OUT. WE WILL
CLAW THE ENEMY. WE WILL DESTROY THE ENEMY.

At this, the three smaller but still freakishly large seagulls cawed excitedly, wild and maniacal screeches of assurance and confidence. Gail did not join in. She caught Flappy's attention with a look of consternation.

WHAT IS IT, MY PET?

The Gull Primus let out several different sounding caws and squawks.

The mutant flock continued to hover, some one hundred feet above the Rock House, as Flappy considered how best to respond.

YES, MY DEAR. THE ENEMY DOES INDEED HAVE
YOUR PRECIOUS GOOFBALL. HE SEEMS TO BE STUCK
TO THE BACK OF THE LARGEST OF THEM—

Gail let out a painful squeak. Flappy cut her off with an emphatic sweep of his right wing.

AND WE WILL TRY OUR BEST TO RESCUE HIM.
HOWEVER, HIS RESCUE CANNOT AND WILL NOT BE
OUR PRIORITY. DEFEATING THE ENEMY MUST COME
FIRST. SHOULD WE LOSE GOOFBALL IN BATTLE, WE
LOSE GOOFBALL IN BATTLE. HE MOST CERTAINLY
WOULDN'T BE THE FIRST GOOFBALL EVER LOST IN
BATTLE, AND SHOULD HE FALL, HE WON'T BE THE
LAST. DO YOU UNDERSTAND, MY DEAR? DO YOU ALL
UNDERSTAND?

The trio of littler birds resumed intense squawking and screeching, the seagull equivalent of a war cry. Gail nodded her head in resignation, determined more than ever the follow the lead of her wise mate. She loved his pragmatism, his logic surrounding Goofball. Flappy truly was the Flappus Maximus.

*DOWN WE FLY. DOWN TO THE GROUND. ONCE
THE BEASTS ARE IN THE BUILDING, WE CHARGE
ON MY COMMAND. THEY WILL NEVER KNOW WHAT
HIT THEM. EXCEPT FOR THE FACT THAT THEY WILL
KNOW THAT BIRDS HIT THEM.*

The birds, led by their confident, gigantic and mutated leader, swooped through the mist down to the parking lot of the Rock House Restaurant. Once on the pavement, they lined up next to the one car – a Tauros mini-convertible electric compact – that was still in the lot. Someone had abandoned the little vehicle, which seemed even smaller next to the Gull Primus and the Flappus Maximus. The roof was down on the convertible and it now looked like a fully filled bathtub on wheels.

The flock was ready, ready to end the fight with the herd, once and for all.

🐂🐂🐂

Once he saw that the gulls had landed and were set to engage in battle, Beefy let fly a series of defiant and insulting moos. In a new development to the bull's mutation, sparks now zapped back and forth between the tips of his horns. The more he mooed, the more he raged. The more he raged, the more intense the sparks became. His glowering purple eyes made the beast look all the more menacing.

As if concerned the birds wouldn't hear his taunting, Beefy added visual insults, sitting down on his haunches and waving his front legs in a wing-like motion as if to say, "Ooh, look at me, I'm a scary bird." The bull stuck out his tongue, offering up a bovine version of a raspberry. "Pffffffffffft." Cow spit flew everywhere.

If Beefy was ever concerned about whether his foes could understand what he was saying, he needn't have worried. They understood. There was only so much a mutated bird could take. Flappy screeched back angrily. A quick squawk to his mate and the gullettes, and the quintet rushed forward.

Clearly, the insults did the trick. The bull was caught off guard by the suddenness of the attack. Luckily there was only room for one of the giant gulls to make it through the doorway at a time, and it was Gail who arrived at the threshold first, leaping forward and smashing right into the face of the mutated bull, both of them tumbling into the building and demolishing the reception area and the first few tables immediately. The Flappus Maximus followed his mate in, the three smaller birds hopping up the rear for added support.

Somewhere deep inside the restaurant, the bird that was being held fast to Kenana's back, Goofball, tried in vain to squawk, "Fly away, it's a trap!" but the mooing, cawing and smashing up of things was just too insanely loud. The others never got the message.

Beefy kicked madly; on his back one second and up and running through the building an instant later. He'd make his way to his feet, launch into an abbreviated death-spin (due to the twelve-foot ceiling) and then dash off, only to be struck by Flappy or Gail, which would cause him to tumble over once again. It was tough for the huge birds to beat their wings enough to fly in the confined space, and they were left to hop and claw, a not totally ineffective but definitely not ideal attack strategy.

Beefy was just trying to buy some time for Kenana, and once he'd passed through the kitchen and behind the bar, destroying both, he'd created some distance between him and his pursuers. He then caught sight of Kenana dropping an explosive pie near the oceanfront windows. The giant cow nodded, and Beefy turned to face the birds, who were hopping gingerly through the broken glass from the previously impressive but now demolished bar. Mahogany panels, pieces of mirror, bits of tables and shattered bottles littered the floor, just as Beefy had hoped. His destructive rampage was doing the job. The bull lowered his head to begin a terror-moo, and the birds stopped in their tracks and began to carefully tippy-talon their way back toward the kitchen. There was too much glass and too low a ceiling for them to do anything else. They had to shield themselves from a direct hit from the deadly moo.

And that's all Beefy had in mind. He just needed a little more time and this wild gull chase would be over. Once the birds were backed into the kitchen, he'd stop the moo and he and Kenana would escape via the back deck.

The terror-moo began, low and vibrating, as Kenana stepped through the doors and out onto the platform, awaiting Beefy as instructed. As the decibel level and tone of the moo rose, the building began to shimmy violently. The birds reached the kitchen, and, just as planned, Beefy stopped mid-call. Mewati took that as her signal, stepped outside and around to the front, and blasted dragon fire at the entryway. Soon, the entire front of the building was an inferno.

Noticing the dragon-cow had done her job, Beefy headed toward the deck, just in time to see it separate from the building, falling away to the rocks below. Lactose Tolerant had gotten confused and had laid down gallons of her acid much too soon, and it had worked too fast. When the vibration of Beefy's terror-moo hit, the combination of the destructive acid and cow call caused complete detachment of the deck, and off it fell. Down the giant cow went, without a sound, just looking at her leader helplessly. Goofball, still stuck like glue to Kenana's back and looking about the size of a parakeet compared to the cow, flapped his wings in vain.

Beefy mooed again, this time in anguish.

Aware that the terror-moo had ceased, the birds were once again making their way through the damaged bar area. But they didn't get far before explosions began to rock the building. Kenana's pie mines were detonating. One after another after another, the blasts shook the restaurant. Dust flew everywhere and the building began to creak in agony, shaking savagely. Like the deck just seconds before, the Rock House Restaurant was coming down.

Due to the swirling dust and the dense smoke from the fire at the front of the building, it was almost impossible for Beefy to see anything. He heard an internal voice, a mutated bovine instinct, scream out for him to head for the light, and he did just that. Faster than he'd ever run before, Beefy charged forward, just as the building began to break away from the side of the cliff. He raced toward the glow of the burning entryway and, as he closed in, he was able to make out just below the flames a gap that had formed as the Rock House broke away from the top of the Bay City plateau. The gap was already a couple of feet wide and getting wider. The sound was deafening, a crunching and rending of wood and metal, as loud and sickening as a banshee's death wail, added to now by the screaming gulls, who had a bird's-eye view of the rocks below as the building tore away. In a frenetic final burst of speed, Beefy leapt, lunging across the gap toward the edge of the cliff. And down the Rock House Restaurant fell, crashing horrifically onto the jagged rocks some three hundred feet below.

The battle was over. And, as is the case with many battles, nobody won.

PART FOUR:

MALICE
AT THE PALACE

N OT TOO LONG AFTER THE Rock House fell, the witnesses to its collapse ducked into the dryness and safety of Ivory Chateaubriand's house, directly across the street from the horrific scene. Ivory introduced everyone to Sir Sanga Loin. The owner of the Blade Barn had followed the assistant deputy's directions to a T, seeking refuge at her place following her orders to evacuate.

"How long ago was that?" Ivory asked herself. "Hours ago? A lifetime ago?"

Devon Steerman interrupted her internal dialogue. "Has anybody seen my dad?"

The group looked around questioningly at one another.

"I thought he was with us," Officer Holstein replied in answer to Devon's question.

Clearly, John Steerman wasn't in attendance.

"The last time I saw him he was sitting on the bench in the park," offered Dr. Herens.

"How's that?" asked Mrs. O'Leary.

The professor reiterated, raising his voice, "I say, the last I saw of John he was sitting on the bench in the park."

"Oh, for certain he's still there," said Margaret confidently. "He'll be wanting to perfect that Sasquatch he's working on."

"You're probably right, Mrs. O'Leary," Devon responded, clearly relieved. "But I think it's supposed to be a yeti."

Sanga Loin looked around the group and offered, "Well on that note, perhaps I should head back to my store. The sun's coming up and the storm seems to have died down, at least for now."

"Be careful out there," Devon cautioned. "This is probably just a break in between storm bands."

Ivory had been trying to get information regarding the storm on her television. None of the channels worked.

"Yes," she said. "If you're headed back, be careful. And remember, we don't know where those cattle went. They could be anywhere."

Loin nodded, grabbing his hat and heading for the door. "I will. And if I see a whittler on a bench I'll let him know where you folks are. Thank you for letting me seek refuge here, Assistant Deputy Chateaubriand. It seems like perhaps I missed quite a show."

"Don't mention it," replied Ivory.

"'Whittler on the Bench.' I love that movie," commented Margaret. She began humming the movie's signature song, "If I Were a Farmhand."

Clarabelle Milken, the hardware store's night manager, stood up. "I guess I'll go with you, Mr. Loin. I need to check out the store, if anything is left of it. Take care, everyone. It's been quite an experience."

Once the two left, Ivory asked, "Can I make some coffee for anyone?"

Devon, the professor, the officer and Margaret all said yes, and several minutes later the group began processing the events that had played out across the street.

Keeping a safe distance, the group had followed the rolling battle as it turned down Braford Street. Once the birds had positioned themselves in the Rock House parking lot, the humans had settled in Ivory's front yard, behind the orange picket fence, directly across the street.

Right off the bat, Ivory had called out, "Oh crap, that's my car! I always park there."

Ivory's mini-convertible was flanked by the two gigantic, mutated gulls. Water was sloshing from the inside of the vehicle out over the doors.

"That's not good," Dr. Herens had suggested, rather redundantly.

The group had stood in stunned silence as Beefy cried out his defiant moo in challenge of the flock, and had gasped as the flying freaks dashed through the front door on top of the bull. It was evident widespread destruction was going on. After several minutes, Lactose Tolerant had appeared from the left side of the building. The restaurant and parking lot lights had made it possible to see fairly well, but when Mewati breathed her dragon-fire, the entire sky lit up.

"What is she doing?" Devon had asked. "Why burn down the restaurant?"

But, despite the flame-improved lighting, nobody could tell. They could only hear the breaking of massive amounts of wood. It was like a lumberjack competition on steroids as the back deck, with Kenana on it, had fallen to the rocks below. Then, above the roar of the fire, they'd heard the sad cry of a bull in distress – Beefy's desperate moo of mourning. Suddenly, explosions had started going off and the birds trapped inside the building began screeching. Their caws were spine-tingling.

Clarabelle had then let out a completely uncontrolled, "Deep sunken ditch!" as if she didn't care who would hear.

Nobody did.

The Rock House lifted and lunged and moaned, ultimately falling prey to Mother Gravity.

Lactose Tolerant and Mewati scurried back and forth in front of the spot that had been the location of the Rock House's front doorway. The two would look over the edge, moo to one another, run around, moo loudly and look over the edge again. The two cows were panic-stricken.

Just over the edge, poor Beefy was just hanging on by his hooves.

The bull's leap across the gap created by the falling building had been partially successful; at least he didn't go down with the steakhouse. But now the situation was precarious to say the least. Beefy had slammed, spread eagle (or spread bull in this case) right onto the newly exposed cliff face, about ten feet down from the level of the parking lot. The horns radiating out low on his legs had pierced right through the rock and held Beefy fast. The bull had climbed about halfway to the top by removing one hoof horn at a time and repositioning it higher up. From the rocks below he must have looked like a sixteen-hundred-pound spider.

Although he'd previously climbed the outside of the Canchim tower with ease, now the mighty, mutated bull was simply out of steam. He was too exhausted to even put one hoof above the other.

The leader of the herd, sensing the dire circumstance he was in, closed his eyes and settled into a deep introspection, recalling a similar time.

I REMEMBER BACK WHEN I WAS BUT A TYKE, NO LARGER THAN CRACKLE. I FELL INTO THE WELL AT THE FARM. I WAS PLAYING WITH THE CHICKENS, JUST AS I'D BEEN CAUTIONED SEVERAL TIMES NOT TO DO. I FORGET THE GAME WE PLAYED. WAS IT BLIND BULL'S BLUFF? KICK THE COW PIE? I DO NOT RECALL. BUT MY OWN ENTHUSIASM GOT THE BETTER OF ME AND I STUMBLED RIGHT DOWN THE WELL.

I SHOULD HAVE DROWNED THAT DAY. I CRIED AND CRIED FOR HOURS. IT WAS ONE OF THE CHICKENS WHO ALERTED THE HUMANS TO MY PREDICAMENT. A CHICKEN WENT UP TO THE KIND WOMAN FROM THE SMALL SHED.

I HEARD THE CHICKEN CLUCK AND CLUCK.

I REMEMBER THE KIND WOMAN ASKING, "WHAT IS IT, GIRL? WHAT IS THE MATTER?"

THEN THE CHICKEN CLUCKED SOME MORE. "CLUCKITY, CLUCK, CLUCK," IT SAID.

AND THEN THE WOMAN ASKED, "WHAT IS IT, GIRL?"

"CLUCK, CLUCK CLUCK CLUCK!"

"WHAT'S THAT?" THE KIND WOMAN ASKED. "BEEFY FELL DOWN THE WELL?"

SOON A ROPE WAS LOWERED INTO THE WELL. SOMEHOW, I WAS LIFTED OUT. WHILE I DON'T RECALL THE METHOD OF MY RESCUE, I RECALL THE RESCUER. IT WAS THE FARMER. IT WAS THE STEER MAN.

THE STEER MAN WAS ALWAYS KIND TO ME. THE STEER MAN WAS MY FRIEND.

I MAY NOT SURVIVE THIS DAY. THE ROCKS ARE A LONG WAY DOWN THERE, AND I CANNOT HANG ON FOREVER.

I MISS THE STEER MAN. I WISH HE WAS HERE, OR IF NOT HIM, AT LEAST THAT CHICKEN. MOO.

Beefy's thoughts were suddenly interrupted by a message that seemed to be playing only inside the bull's brain: *"YOU HAVE BEEN CHOSEN. APPROACH THE PALACE. COME TO THE PALACE."*

The message repeated.

Back at parking lot level, Mewati the dragon-cow located Beefy, turned around and slowly and carefully backed up, scooching right to the edge of the cliff. She lowered her metallic tail down over the edge, squatting her hind end low so as to give Beefy better access. The bull, imbedded in the cliff face by the claws on his legs, stretched his neck with all his might and snapped his teeth, trying to chomp down on Mewati's tail. But he was missing the tip by inches.

His massive horns were visible from the parking lot; they jutted up past the cliff's edge. But his would-be rescuers had no hands so they couldn't grab the enormous tusk-like appendages to pull Beefy up to safety. Lactose Tolerant even squatted and tried to cup her front hooves around one of the horns, to no avail. She just couldn't do it. The cow looked over the edge. Beefy was sweating profusely and his purple eyes looked both serious and panicked at the same time.

Lactose Tolerant let out a desperate moo, a bovine plea for a miraculous rescue.

"Should we try and help?" asked Devon.

The group of humans, drawn by the desperate mooing, was now watching the drama unfold from behind Ivory's water-logged Tauros.

The professor patted his student on the shoulder consolingly, replying, "No, son. It's nature's way."

Just then, a loud clanking and scraping sound began down Braford Street and out of the early morning darkness came the three little cows, running as usual at breakneck speed. Huey, Curly and Crackle all carried in their shark-like teeth a long steel cable. Pulled from the giant dumpster where they'd been foraging, the cable was plenty long and would be able to reach down to the cliff-hanging Beefy. It took all three of the little beasts to carry the thing and, though they wobbled, crashed and stumbled every few feet, the trio had heeded the moos of their aunts and come to the rescue. They veered around Ivory's car and headed straight for the now-prostrate Mewati and Lactose Tolerant.

The large cows laid low on the pavement and extended their necks, and the three amigos wound and wrapped the center section of cable around them, tight enough to be snug, but not strangle. Crackle mooed what appeared to be instructions, and the cows stood up, facing the front of the lot. Curly and Huey each grabbed an end of the cable in their teeth and dropped it over the edge on top of Beefy. The bull chomped onto both of the cable termini and shook his head violently, back and forth, and soon the cable strands were a jumbled mess, tangled tightly between his giant horns. Sparks crackled between his horn tips. Beefy let out a triumphant moo, addressing the two large cows.

Mewati and Lactose Tolerant stood up and started walking. Their pull was all Beefy needed to hoist himself back to level ground.

Mrs. O'Leary let out a raucous "Right on!" and the rest of the group of observing humans clapped and hugged one another.

All were clearly relieved by the successful rescue.

The mutated farm animals appeared to have no time for such pleasantries. As soon as he was on all four hooves, Beefy started mooing out instructions to his charges. Looking from cow to cow intently as if to gauge understanding, the bull mooed on. When he finished, the herd turned as one, looking directly at the folks lined up behind the soggy vehicle. Then the animals took off, sprinting away from the cliff with purpose, back the way they'd come.

I AM SADDENED BY THE LOSS OF KENANA. SHE GAVE HER LIFE TO SAVE OURS. I AM STILL BEEFY. MY PURPOSE SHALL BE FULFILLED.

LISTEN NOW, MY HERD. I SHALL MOO IN SLOW AND CONCISE WORDS. KENANA'S LIFE SHALL NOT HAVE BEEN IN VAIN. I HAVE RECEIVED A MESSAGE, A MESSAGE OF HOPE, A MESSAGE OF DIRECTION.

AS I HUNG, SUSPENDED AND VULNERABLE, I RECEIVED A MOST URGENT COMMUNICATION. IT BORE INTO MY BRAIN, WHERE IT RESIDES EVEN STILL. A CONTINUAL, REPEATING LOOP.

IT SAYS, "YOU HAVE BEEN CHOSEN. APPROACH THE PALACE. COME TO THE PALACE."

OVER AND OVER THE MESSAGE PLAYS. I HAVE BEEN CHOSEN, AND TOGETHER WE SHALL RUN. WE SHALL RUN TO THE PALACE, THE PALACE FOR COWS. NONE SHALL STOP US. MOO, MOO MOO MOO.

The motivated cattle raced down Braford Street and, once they got to its intersection with Lineback Street, found in dawn's early light that the business boulevard didn't stop there, but instead continued north down what was commonly called "the crookedest street in the West." Back and forth the animals tore down the switchbacks, the three crazy calves even giving out the mooing equivalent of joyous "whees" as they banked around each turn. The larger animals had fun descending the crooked road as well, but had too much dignity to moo about it.

The Lineback switchbacks ended at Enderby Island Boulevard. "E.I.," as the locals called it, eventually headed smack-dab into the center of the Financial District, but not before it traveled through the Wharf District.

The twelve-block tourist destination, known as Fishyman's Wharf, was named after Bay City's first mayor, Gyr Fishyman. The district was right on the water, adjacent to Bay City Bay. It was a destination popular with tourists because of its vibrant fishing, sightseeing, windsurfing and historic prison industries. The Bay City Police Department precinct where Officer Holstein had reported the floating purple menace had been located in this thriving commercial area. Had been, but was not any longer.

For when the Contented Corners creatures sloshed their way through the area, there was no more Fishyman's Wharf.

During the battle on Lineback Street, many areas of Bay City were suffering significant damage at the hands of Typhoon Bessie. Landslides ravaged the hilly metropolis. Tornadoes, similar to the one that touched down at the Cow Palace, appeared out of nowhere, destroyed buildings here and there, and then simply vanished. Lightning struck and blasted trees, transformers and tall towers, sometimes to smithereens. And while Mother and Mutant Nature both battered the city by the bay, it was the bay itself that caused the most extensive destruction. Bay City Bay destroyed Fishyman's Wharf.

The sequential storm surges that flooded both Contented Corners and the nearby university were much more severe in the Wharf District. The ocean inlet to the large bay, spanned by the iconic Big Bridge, intensified the push of water propelled by the typhoon's high winds. The water level of the bay rose quickly, swiftly topping the six-foot-tall protective sea wall and overwhelming some of the most popular tourist destinations on the West Coast.

The bayside Golden Steak Park, with its spectacular Ongole Reddenbaker Popcorn Gardens, was gone in an instant, destroyed by a wall of water that didn't seem to care who or what it hurt. Next destroyed were a half a dozen of the world famous Bay City trolley cars, tossed about and mangled in their storage pen like so many rubber baby buggies.

In a bizarre demolition with unexpected consequences, Pier 22's Bay City Aquarium, a popular site for school field trips, was carried out into the bay. The aquarium was located inside of several railroad cars positioned side by side on the massive wooden pier, and when the water rushed in, the small buildings simply floated away. Once fully saturated, the cars sank to the bottom of the bay and the thousands of fish that had been located in the dozens of aquariums swam off, most likely unaware they were in the center of a gigantic freak storm.

The district's sporting venues were not exempt from the wrath of the rushing water, as both the Latvian Brown Memorial Drag Strip, and the quaint Xingjiang Flying Disc Stadium were wiped clean, as if with a giant squeegee, while the flood raged and a ten-foot-deep river flowed along the E.I.

Bakeries renowned for their production of sweet and sour dough bread, such as the massive Santa Cruz Baguette and Laundry and the Pie Rouge des Plaines Bakery and Auto Repair Shop, were washed away as well.

Sadly, so was the building that housed Precinct Seventeen of the Bay City Police Department.

Local resources were stretched to the limit by the sudden and intense fury of the deadly storm. There weren't enough first responders on duty and most of those who were had to shelter in place because the wind and rain were so severe. The water started rushing into the precinct building within minutes of the storm's beginning and, before the phone lines went dead, the few officers on hand had received more than enough emergency calls to hit Code Black status. So many people needed assistance that everyone who had been in the building, including Staff Sergeant Jones, who had assisted Officer Holstein hours earlier, was out on a call by the time the second storm surge hit, lifting the building off its foundation and tearing it to pieces.

ᘉᕦᘉ ᘉᕦ ᘉᕦᘉ

Had there been more of them, the herd would have looked like a real Western movie stampede as they ran down the muddy E.I. and out of the decimated Wharf District. They rumbled on east toward the tall buildings in the heart of the city, a portion of the metropolis that appeared miraculously undamaged by the worst storm in history.

In actuality, miracles had nothing to do with the lack of destruction. It was money that saved the Financial District. This part of the city was not protected by a mere six-foot sea wall, as was the case at Fishyman's Wharf. No, a massive, golden, thirty-foot-tall concrete barrier, adorned with huge gargoyle statues across the top, protected the downtown area – and its billionaires – from the storm surges Bessie tossed at it. The five-hundred-million-dollar barrier had dollar signs etched into its bay-facing side, announcing to steamships and island prison tourists that this section was off-limits – unless you had money to invest.

Dozens of skyscrapers lined the main thoroughfare, towering above Enderby Island Boulevard as it shot like an arrow through the heart of the district. It was these massive structures that shielded the streets below from the torrential rain and ripping winds. While the tall buildings were buffeted and battered by the typhoon, down on E.I. a light sprinkling of rain was all that could be felt. Most of the bankers, stock brokers, insurance agents and other money-related professionals who worked in the city center didn't realize, as they headed off to work, that, over the last several hours, the rest of the city had been under attack from wind, rain, cows and birds. Sure, cell service was out, as were local radio and television stations, but money had to be made. Somebody would fix the phones. Somebody would report the latest news. It was time to get to work.

The Financial District was densely packed with people seven days a week. And though the sun had just risen, and it was a Sunday morning, a myriad of money-focused folks were scattered about, a great many of them on the streets, in coffee shops, bicycling about or just trying to get to work. All were intent on making it to their respective cubicles.

Beefy and his charges were no less motivated and, seeing as how the palace for cows was on the other side of the Financial District from the animals, something was going to have to give, and give soon. The bull continued to keep a rapid pace, and once out of the decimated Wharf District he looked up. He could see massive buildings and people walking back and forth on sidewalks just a few blocks ahead. He let out a moo and charged forth, faster still.

I THINK IT IS TIME TO FLY ALONG. I HAVE HAD ENOUGH OF THESE CREATURES WITH THE HORNS AND THE BURNING LIQUID AND THE FLAMES. I AM THE FLAPPUS MAXIMUS AND I MUST ACT IN THE BEST INTEREST OF MY FLOCK. THE LITTLE ONES, SNAP, MOE AND LOUIE, WERE SO FRIGHTENED BY THE FIGHT UPON THE CLIFF. I KNEW WE HAD THE BEASTS WHERE WE WANTED THEM, BUT WE WERE THE UNLUCKY VICTIMS OF BAD TIMING, BEING INSIDE THE BUILDING WHEN IT EXPLODED. IT WAS NO LARGE THING TO PROTECT THE FLOCK, INCLUDING MY DEAR GULL PRIMUS, WITHIN THE COCOON OF MY BATTLE-WINGS. I WRAPPED THEM ALL TIGHT AND HELD THEM CLOSE AS THE BUILDING FELL AND CRASHED UPON THE ROCKS.

I REMAIN UNCERTAIN AS TO HOW GOOFBALL ESCAPED INJURY FROM THE FALL AND HOW HE MANAGED TO GET AWAY FROM THE DEATH-GRIP OF THE ENORMOUS MUTANT. PERHAPS THAT ONE'S INJURIES INCLUDED THE SHORT-CIRCUITING OF ITS EVIL ADHESION FIELD. BUT SURVIVE GOOFBALL DID, AND TOGETHER AGAIN WE ARE, AND IT IS TIME TO LEAVE THIS HORRID AND UNLUCKY PLACE.

FOR BATTLES I CAN FIGHT, FOREVER IF NEEDED. I AM THE FLAPPUS MAXIMUS. BAD LUCK I CANNOT FIGHT. IT CAN NEVER BE A FAIR FIGHT TO FIGHT BAD LUCK. SO, FLY MY FLOCK, FLY. INTO THE SUNRISE, AND THE LESS BAD LUCK-FILLED VALLEY THAT LIES AHEAD. AN ETERNITY OF FLAT AND PAVED SURFACES WITH UNLIMITED GARBAGE AWAITS. AN ENDLESS SUBURBIA OF SHOPPING MALLS. AND BEYOND THAT, A PARADISE OF PESTICIDES, RIPE FOR OUR TESTING. FLY TO THE SUNRISE MY FLOCK, FLY!

Kenana's injuries were massive. The mutated double-cow suffered broken bones all over. More than a half dozen of her stomachs had been injured. The poor girl's tail was broken in two places, and she'd bit her tongue upon her crash-landing, turning what should have been her mooing cries into lisping whispers of pain.

The beast would have no doubt succumbed to the injuries if it hadn't been for two fortunate and previously undiscovered mutations. First, salt water actually healed the cow. It acted in a manner similar to the Flappus Maximus' spit and its amazing mutated seagull-healing properties. For Kenana the infusion of water, ironically the same water that had carried the radiation-laded debris pile to the West Coast in the first place, repaired her broken bones and healed her wounded stomachs.

Also, Kenana's adhesion field had previously only ever acted like a huge sheet of flypaper – or, as the case had shown, bird paper – and the only thing that could counteract it appeared to be a direct shot from a stun gun. But, as Kenana learned while she was falling at terminal velocity toward the jagged rocks, the energy field on her back could also repel objects away from her in a more traditional force field manner. This second new mutation had not only flung Goofball to safety during the rapid descent, but had protected Kenana from having the flaming restaurant fall directly on top of her broken body. Instead, the gigantic heap of burning debris was pushed as it fell, landing up against the cliff face and missing the cow by several feet.

Kenana had been unconscious for about an hour, but the massive beast eventually was able to open her eyes. Broken boards from the deck were scattered everywhere. Kenana's legs and tail were in the water but the rest of her body was on the rocks. She was facing west, toward the tip of the peninsula. She couldn't move, in another irony, similar to Officer Holstein and later Goofball, when they had been trapped on the cow's back. So, for a while, she lay there, breathing slowly and healing, looking out to the west. The cow went in and out of consciousness. In yet another irony, two non-mutated seagulls landed on Kenana's side, basking in the sunrise.

After a while, across the horizon, small moving dots appeared. They gradually took on shapes as they came closer. It was people, a lot of people, on boards. Some of them stood and propelled themselves with long paddles. Others laid flat on their boards and kicked and swam forward. And in their midst was another being, much larger than the humans. A four-legged wonder standing upon a large metal door was being propelled forward by several swimmers. Purple eyes covered in a red bandana, bright muumuu around her waist. Kenana knew who it was: Mrs. Beefy was coming to her rescue.

The cow let out a weak moo. The birds on its back cawed. The sun rose.

ᐦ ᐦ ᐦ

Tom McDonald had spent an entire career as a part-time professional crossing guard. He'd guided children, old ladies, dogs and even other off-duty crossing guards across streets all over Bay City for decades. Old Tom, as the locals called him, would never be seen without his handy and somewhat weathered STOP sign. A little frayed around the edges and a bit faded despite more than a dozen re-paintings, the sign was his most trusted companion.

These days Tom guarded crosswalks just for fun. Though retired, he still crossed folks on a volunteer basis, as a hobby. It kept him busy. Most every morning he could be found escorting the money people and merchants back and forth across Enderby Island Boulevard as they headed to and from their destinations in the heart of the Bay City Financial District. He'd do this for about an hour, then catch the bus back to where he lived in the Bayside neighborhood. Before walking home he'd stop in at the local coffee place, the Cow Town Latte House, and order The Usual. He'd sit and tell folks about his experiences from his morning in "the Big Bay City," as he called it. Most days, a half dozen or so other regulars were on hand as Tom related, and embellished, the events of the morning. He had an unusual way of describing things, and that just added to the uniqueness of what was known as the "Daily Old Tom McDonald Yarn."

For example, Tom wouldn't call animals by their actual names, he'd call them by the sound they make. A horse was "whinny," and two horses were called "whinny whinny." It took some getting used to, but was no stranger than when the storyteller called politicians by the tree they most resembled or countries by the food common to the region.

"Blue Cypress went to pizza," was something Tom McDonald would say from time to time, before adding, "I wonder who he got to feed those arf arf of his."

Eventually, people got used to this, and even looked forward to the challenge of deciphering Tom's tales.

The day after the typhoon hit, Tom was particularly excited to tell the regulars about the morning's wild adventure, and he was disappointed to find only the barista, Blaarkop, whose friends just called him Blaar, in the place.

Tom walked up to the counter. "Where is everyone?" he asked.

"Didn't you hear?" replied the surprised barista. "The storm, it wiped about everything out. I wouldn't have bothered opening if it wasn't for the fact I live upstairs."

Tom had spent the night at his sister's apartment in downtown Bay City. He didn't know about the storm.

"Well that could explain things," he said.

"Explain what, Mr. McDonald?" asked Blaar.

"Well, since nobody is here, why don't we get some coffee and we can sit and I'll tell you all about it," suggested Tom.

"Sounds fine," replied the coffee maker. "You want The Usual?"

"No, after today I need an extra jolt. Let's go for the Calf-fiend Explosion."

The half-coffee, half-milk drink featured four shots of espresso. It was the place's signature latte.

"Coming right up!" said Blaarkop excitedly. He'd never been front and center for one of Tom's stories before, always hearing them from behind the counter and getting the gist of things in bits and pieces.

A couple of minutes later, the two men were sitting across from each other, and Tom McDonald, his trusty sign set safely atop a nearby table, spun his yarn.

"Well, first off, in my eighty-plus years, I thought I'd seen it all. But today was even crazier than the time Redwood Tree tried to send troops into artichoke."

Blaarkop sipped his hot beverage. *"This might be tough to follow, but should be a good diversion,"* he thought.

The retired but still somewhat active professional crossing guard looked up at the ceiling, as if searching for the best way to begin.

"Enderby Island Boulevard. I was working there, crossing folks. You know where I mean?"

"I'm not sure," replied Blaar.

Tom remembered nobody used the full name of the street anymore. "E.I."

"E.I.? Oh," Blaar said, "the main road in town." He nodded his understanding.

Tom continued. "Well there I am, crossing folks back and forth, and I look west and here comes this big herd, headed straight at me. I mean, there I am in the middle of the road. And next thing I know there is a moo moo here, a moo moo there. Here a moo, there a moo, everywhere a moo moo. Right in the middle of town. But these weren't regular moo moo. They were warped. Something awful had happened to them. And they just came charging ahead."

Blaarkop thought he was following the story. He chastised himself for not having sat in on an Old McDonald Yarn before.

Tom took a big gulp of his Calf-fiend Explosion and continued. "Money people and merchants were running everywhere. It was total chaos. One moo had gigantic horns and tossed cars up in the air like they were tiny toy cars. Luckily, I was escorted into a bank by a kind lady or I would have been trampled by the roar-moo." (Blaarkop wasn't exactly sure what that meant.) "These three little snarl-moo moo were running all around, and I saw this one moo shoot some green goo out of her and it dissolved a delivery van right in half!" Tom drank some more coffee. He went on. "There are two giant statues in front of the stock exchange, one of a bear and one of a bull."

Blaarkop noticed that Tom called statues of animals by their correct animal names. *"Odd,"* he thought. And then he realized if that was the only thing odd about this story, he just might need to see a psychiatrist as his ex-wife had suggested. Tom was still talking. *"I'd better pay attention,"* the coffee server thought.

"So, when they get to the statue of the bull, the moo moo all gather around it and bow down, like some sorta ceremony, and then off they run again. It was horrible, I tell you. I mean, you know that country where people flock every year to swim with the moo moo and, as it turns out, its dangerous and people get hurt or killed?"

Blaarkop nodded. He'd heard about the Swimming of the Bulls in Spanish Europe, and thought that perhaps someday he'd love to give it a try. Then again, perhaps his ex-wife was right after all and he needed professional help.

"If you got in their way, the moo moo would run you over, light you on fire, chomp into your leg or dissolve you in acid. It was smart to get out of the way. Sadly, several people didn't get out of the way. They never knew what hit them." Tom completed his story. "I tell you, I'm no coward, but I got out of there as soon as I saw an opening. The last I saw, the big moo was tossing a taxi cab over the top of a city bus."

Blaarkop shook his head and wondered where the animals had headed once they'd destroyed the Financial District. He had a lot of questions to ask the kindly, odd man, but before he could query, McDonald took a final swig of his coffee, stood up and moved toward the door.

"Thanks for the coffee. I'm headed out," he said. "I think I'll go mow the lawn." And out the door he went.

"He sure has a lot of energy," Blaar thought. The coffee connoisseur shook his head in reflection. *"That was certainly a story you don't hear every day."* Blaarkop felt fairly confident he understood most of what had transpired in the Financial District, and it wasn't good.

From what he could tell, mutated, stampeding, rampaging cattle had blasted through the city center, and there was probably extensive damage, and dead and injured people. The tall buildings had kept the storm at bay, but not the cows. Who could blame them? They were only buildings.

ᏇᎦ ᏇᎦ ᏇᎦ

"Will you watch over my yeti?"

It was quite a touching scene when John Steerman handed off his creation to Margaret O'Leary for safekeeping.

"How's that?" Margaret asked kindly, still holding Chicken One under her left arm and slipping the small carving into a front pocket of her rain slicker.

John tipped the brim of his imaginary cowboy hat and said, "Ma'am." He climbed into the driver side of his pickup.

The aardvarks slept in the truck bed.

"I guess that's it," announced Officer Holstein. "We're off then." He slid into the truck and sat next to Devon, who had already scooted in next to his father.

A few minutes earlier, John Steerman drove up, having been pointed in the correct direction by Clarabelle Milken and Sanga Loin, who had found him still seated on the Aceh Park bench, whittling away. After a short group discussion, the decision was made that John and Devon Steerman, along with Officer Holstein, would head off in pursuit of the cows. Ivory, Professor Herens and Margaret would stay back to clean up and help with whatever they could. Ivory was particularly worried about the status of the baby animals back at the Calfeteria. All agreed that it was probably best if the trio checked not only on the little critters, but everyone else that may be stuck at or returning to Lineback Street.

Professor Herens was deciding whether to say "good luck" or "hang in there" when the farmer started up the old Tauros truck's engine and took off to look for Beefy and the cows.

Once John certified that the herd hadn't doubled back down Lineback Street, there was only one way the mutants could have gone: down the switchbacks.

It was a glorious morning in Bay City. The storm bands Devon had warned Sir Loin about had moved on. Scattered clouds and a brilliant blue sky greeted the men as the truck slowly descended the wildly winding street, and for a moment it was possible to believe that this was just another perfect Sunday in Bay City. Typhoon Bessie dissipated as quickly as it had formed, and Bay City Bay sparkled brightly, glittering below the massive Big Bridge. The pavement was wet but not slippery or dangerous along the switchbacks, and everything looked as it should; until the street ended in a tee at E.I.

Officer Holstein noticed it first and let out a loud gasp. "Oh no," he said.

John turned right at the intersection. He stopped in the middle of the street, turned off the engine and climbed out, plopping down onto the pavement. Devon and the policeman followed suit, and all three gazed at the destruction in silence, stunned to discover that Fishyman's Wharf, the entire district it seemed, was gone.

It was easy to tell which direction the horrific herd had gone once they hit the north end of Lineback Street. They'd avoided the western route that led to the iconic bridge and had turned right, heading into the decimated tourist area. Hoofprints from the beasts were all over the mud that was several inches thick across the road. Three sets of these prints headed east in a direct line, no doubt laid down by Beefy, Mewati and Lactose Tolerant. The three little creatures left their tracks in the mud as well, but these veered every which way, owing to Curly, Huey and Crackle's penchant for crazy galloping.

But there were no buildings left – anywhere. This wasn't cow damage. It was storm damage. Typhoon Bessie had wiped Fishyman's Wharf off the map.

"The precinct!" called out Officer Holstein as he sprinted down the road, adding his footprints to the bovine-created ones in the mud.

He made it about fifty yards and stopped, bending halfway over and resting his hands on his knees. He began to sob. Within a few minutes, Devon and John had slogged their way to the grieving man; Devon patting the officer on his right shoulder, John secretly wishing he hadn't given away his yeti.

"It's gone," sobbed Officer Holstein. "It's all gone."

He didn't need to say more. He was right, it was all gone.

A half an hour later they were back in the pickup, heading east toward downtown and the Financial District. Their wish was that things would be better there, with the tall buildings hopefully protecting citizens from the full force of the storm. How right they were, yet at the same time, how very wrong.

ᐸᑫᔑᐸᑫᔑᐸᑫᔑ

"YOU HAVE BEEN CHOSEN. APPROACH THE PALACE. COME TO THE PALACE."

The parking lot beacon sent out a signal meant to be heard by only one creature on the planet: Beefy.

Up and down, the center post protruding out of the cylindrical base moved, emitting a loud ping at its apex. The multi-colored lights that adorned the humming machine continued to flash.

"What do you think it is?" asked the biker, Han.

Of all questions that have ever been asked that have been rhetorical, this one was probably the most. How could any of them have known what it was?

The humorous Brad, cow head gripped tightly in his right hand, jokingly said, "It's probably an interstellar electrical lint roller."

He chuckled nervously. Nobody else did. Lint roller indeed.

On the other hand, or other hoof as the case may be, Beefy knew exactly what the strange machine was. It was a beacon. A signal, boring straight into the bull's every fiber. A repeating message that said, *"YOU HAVE BEEN CHOSEN. APPROACH THE PALACE. COME TO THE PALACE."*

He led the herd out of the Financial District and without incident through the Bayview District. Just a handful of citizens, including one old man who was mowing his lawn, witnessed the mutated herd's eastern charge. Beefy slowed the pace a bit and looked on adoringly as they passed the Cow Town Latte House, as if he wanted to head inside for a cup of java. Offering up a wink and a moo, the beast was off again, racing down several iconic Bay City streets on his way to his ultimate goal.

Down Albera Street, famous for its antique fishing pole shops, the herd headed. Straight through the Pineapple Upside Down Cake neighborhood they ran. They galloped along the fence that lined the Pajama Golf Course, where the unusual dress code for participants was strictly enforced. Down Balancer Boulevard, past the Aure et Saint-Girons puppy wig factory, and through the Indo-Brazilian park and the site of the 1934 Bingo Olympic Games the herd ran.

Eventually Beefy led the beasts onto the gently descending Guzerat Street. And before too long their destination appeared on the right: the Cow Palace.

Power had been restored to the area and the massive electronic sign at the entrance flashed "CAR SALE TODAY" in giant, white letters. Beefy couldn't read, but if he could, one look at the sign and a quick glance down into the mangled mess in the parking lot and he perhaps would have mooed menacingly, *"THERE WILL BE NO CAR SALE HERE TODAY."*

Back in the lot, the men standing and contemplating the beacon couldn't see the approaching herd as they were located around the corner of the arena from the parking lot entrance.

The cow mascot was facing north and first saw the beasts charge around the corner. He did what any other bovine-dressed person would do in that situation. Brad pointed at the onrushing herd and yelled out, "COWS!"

ᙡᙢ ᙡᙢ ᙡᙢ

First responders, stretched to their limits and scattered all about Bay City, were just starting to arrive at Enderby Island Boulevard in the heart of the Financial District. John, Devon and Chris could hear the sirens as the trio headed up several steps and stood amidst the devastation, scanning the large plaza area in front of the Tharparker Bank. The walking wounded had congregated here. People burned by acid or flame and folks gored or zapped by Beefy's horns sat on benches or were laid out near a large fountain.

A couple of people were trying their best to provide emergency care, and once they caught sight of the uniformed Officer Holstein they called out, "We could use some help over here!"

Without hesitation, all three of the gentlemen dashed over to give whatever assistance they could. Holstein, among his many other talents, was well-versed in first aid and could at least head up an initial triage process until the EMTs arrived several minutes later. John and Devon dashed back and forth, getting requested supplies out of the bank, which fortunately had an impressive emergency cache in the basement.

Once the professionals arrived, the farmer and his son decided they should continue on in search of their cattle. They headed back to the pickup. Officer Holstein, the only representative of the Bay City Police Department on hand, decided to stay at the scene. The last the Steermans saw of him, Officer Holstein was suggesting to a fire department official that he thought a complete evacuation of the Financial District would be in order.

Down on E.I., the carnage was sickening. Fires burned in the lobbies of several buildings. Vehicles were tossed about, many half-melted or burned-out. A trio of Beefy's terror-moos had shattered every street-level window and glass shards were everywhere. Several fire hydrants had been sheared off, shooting geysers high into the air. John had to zig and zag the pickup through the scattered wreckage, but eventually he and Devon made it east into the Bayview District.

From there, the herd's trail, though it caromed through the east side of Bay City, was fairly easy to trace. All John had to do was follow the garbage. Huey, Curly and Crackle had managed to shred every trashcan they ran across in their constant and voracious hunt for cooked meats.

Twenty minutes later, as John turned onto Guzerat Street, Devon exclaimed, "Of course! Why didn't I figure this out before?"

From their position, they could see the top of the roof of the Cow Palace arena.

"It's the Cow Palace, Dad. The cows went to the Cow Palace!"

"Yep," replied John. "I suppose so. I reckon it's time to bring 'em on home."

ᓂᓄ ᓂᓄ ᓂᓄ

THE HUMANS. THEY ARE IN THE WAY.

Beefy knew this for certain. He needed to get his herd to the beacon, The Source, as Beefy had come to call it, and these people were blocking his path. Certainly, they looked startled, and that lent credence to the bull's previous thought that humans were clueless rather than evil, like the mutated gulls. Still, Beefy needed to get them out of the way. They were both meddlesome and problematic.

The herd leader lowered his head to begin a terror-moo, but stopped even before the ground started shaking. He didn't want to damage The Source. He wasn't sure what to do. A death-spin seemed to be pointless. With sparks zipping back and forth between his horn tips and purple eyes glowing, Beefy pawed his right hoof onto the pavement, an international bull signal to charge. Behind him, the two large beasts and three panting, smaller creatures pawed at the parking lot asphalt as well. It was "go time."

Salers Salorn jumped into action. He dashed in front of the surprised group of humans and began swishing his magnificent cape back and forth, grabbing the attention of the entire herd. He let out a loud wooting sound, sort of like an owl with a megaphone, and calmly turned and began backing up, carefully heading toward the rear end of the building. He'd swish, woot and step back, and the mutants followed along, as if caught in a tractor beam of swishing. Before long the bullfighter and the bovines were nearly to the far corner of the arena.

Siri Batangas, in full impersonator form, was the first of the rest of the group to speak. "I just wanna say, Momma, that there bullfighter can't keep this up alone. I-I-I mean, I don't know what his game is, but we all gotta help. Ya know what I mean?"

With that, he dashed off into the RV and, in a surprisingly short time, came out dressed in a sequined white lamé jumpsuit. He had a long white sash around his neck and a bejeweled and gilded show cape folded over one arm.

He gave a quick nod to the five other folks and dashed back to the rear of the building calling out, "Thank you. Thank you very much."

Shorty let out a panicked sort of a gasp. "Okay, what in the world is going on?"

It was Red who spoke up, inspired by the sudden action of the bullfighter and celebrity impersonator. "I think I can explain things clearly."

The Henchman, Brad the mascot, Shorty and Han stood with rapt attention, like steers staring down a rodeo clown.

The car dealer clarified the situation as best he could. "Look, that giant butter churn must have come here from the government. They launched it and it landed here. How, I do not know. Probably it crashed. Anyway, those lights and sounds are clearly some sort of homing device, and those monsters, I guess cowsters would be a better word, need at that butter churn. Our job, as that bullfighter character musta figgered out, is to keep the cowsters from the butter churn."

"But, why?" asked a confused The Henchman. It seemed like a reasonable question to him. "Why don't we just get out of the way?"

"And what?" asked a suddenly irate Red. "Offer them some tea? Look, these things are hell-bent on destruction, and that butter churn is key to them doing that somehow. Now, we're gonna do things my way." He then shouted, "Anybody got a problem with that?"

Nobody did.

"Good, let's move it. We need to act and act fast."

He dashed off, leading the group toward the west end of the Cow Palace and the main entry, and there he laid out his plan of action.

"Shorty, Han, you guys get on your bikes and get to the back lot. Distraction is the key here. While we agree..."

Red was staring now right at Dutch. The Henchman's eyes began to dart about.

"We *all* agree that we need to keep the cowsters away from the entire RV area, how we do that isn't exactly clear. I say we distract and move. Distract and move. Like a boxer, except we're not boxers."

"How do we win a fight if we distract and move?" asked Brad. A reasonable question to him.

Red looked at Brad. Brad put on his cow head.

Red erupted again. "I'll tell you how now, brown cow." (Brad's cow costume was indeed brown in color.) "We distract and move them until we are safely far enough away to give one of these bike riders a chance to go call the National Army. That's how. They may need to go nuclear on these bastards."

Brad was convinced this was more than likely an exaggeration, but nodded his large cow head in agreement. "How can I help?" he asked.

"You can catch a ride with one of these two and get to the back of this place, as in right now, and just help out those two brave entertainers who aren't standing around talking, but who are actually doing something. We're here talking, and they're distracting monsters. You get the picture?"

"So, just head back and act like a cow?" asked Brad.

Red then began some of the most creative cursing any of the group had ever heard, and soon the bikers were headed off, the cow mascot sharing Shorty's bike and hanging on for dear life as they zoomed around the corner of the building.

Red turned and faced Dutch. "That leaves just you and me, The Henchman. Help me grab those horns."

The duo bent to pick up the massive horns that had been mounted on the front grill of Simford's oversized Tauros, but had been knocked off when the well-intentioned men tried to ram through the front entry doors of the arena.

"I assume Ol' Longhorn still runs," Red added.

Friesian certainly hoped it did.

At the back of the building, Salers Salorn and Siri Batangas had managed to get on either side of the small herd and were leading the beasts out toward the far east end of the parking lot. The bullfighter didn't really have any plan in mind, as Red had surmised. Things were far simpler for him. He was a bullfighter and Beefy was a bull. Salers was born to swish. He could keep this up for hours.

Siri, however, had never used his cape to distract bulls before, and was used to donning the garb for the finale of his act, typically in a nightclub setting. As it turned out, the impressionist had quite a knack for cape swishing, and he just followed the expert Salers' lead. Though he probably could have pulled it off, the professional impersonator decided he couldn't effectively woot like the Spanish European. He hadn't had the opportunity to study the nuances of proper bullfighter wooting and wasn't about to improvise. Siri Batangas would not simply woot willy-nilly. He did, after all, have a reputation to uphold. So, he had to create his own call of distraction. Siri would swish, yell out "hunka hunka," and step.

It seemed to be working, as the beasts had formed a defensive circle, mooing, roaring and snarling as the men danced the dance of distraction in and around the wreckage of dozens of automobiles on a bright, sunny Bay City Sunday morning. The chaos was almost serene.

The addition of a couple of bikers and a dancing cow mascot complicated matters instantly. Shorty and Han zipped and zagged tauntingly through the proceedings. Brad climbed up on the roof of a severely damaged Tauros stretch limousine and began to dance, chanting "MOO MOO MOO MOO" in quite hilarious fashion. It was easy to see why Herbie the Heifer was in such high demand.

While the addition of these distractions to the previous distractions succeeded in breaking up the herd circle, it also managed to get them fairly riled up. Thinking, *I DON'T HAVE*

TIME FOR THIS! Beefy mooed out the bovine equivalent of "*FIGHT*" to his charges and they all went into a frenzy.

Frenzy meant different things to different mutants, and in the case of Lactose Tolerant it meant line up and fire her now-precise acid streams. She focused her attacks on the bullfighter, but he was just too fast, and every time she turned to position her body for a broadside shot, Salorn would dash to her front, swishing and wooting and stepping. And the Spanish European was not the only one who excelled at his craft. Mewati went straight for the two bikers, roaring and blasting fire every which way, but they too eluded the frantic fire-breather at every blast. It appeared at first as though Huey, Crackle and Curly leapt straight for Brad, and he was quite alarmed at the sight of the onrushing mini-terrors, but they went zooming past the limo and straight down a loading dock, smashing into a half a dozen overflowing trashcans.

Beefy looked out at the mayhem, a tough task because every swish of Siri's cape seemed to grab his attention like the world's most powerful tractor beam tugging on a spoon.

THIS IS GETTING NOWHERE. IF IT WASN'T FOR THIS CONTINUAL DISTRACTION I COULD GORE OR TRAMPLE THESE HUMANS AND GET BACK TO THE SOURCE. ENOUGH!

The beast let out a long and defiant moo. His purple eyes pulsed and his horn tips sparked. He began a terror-moo. Low at first, completely inaudible until it rose in level to a rumble. The wrecked cars began to bounce up and down. The fighting was close, near enough to Beefy that a full-blown terror-moo would, at the very least, stun the humans, knocking them back, at which point their defeat would be a foregone conclusion. The horrific moo rose in key and began to morph into a sickening howl.

The noise of the howling, motorbikes, roars, snarls, mascot moos, hunka hunkas and woots was deafening. And yet, above all the din, a loud and familiar voice rang out.

"COWS, TO ME!"

It was John Steerman. He called out again, his voice amplified by Professor Herens' bullhorn, set to full blast.

"COWS, TO ME!"

At once all of the cattle, including the little terrors on the loading dock, turned to face the farmer. The mayhem instantly stopped and the herd slowly and obediently headed toward the owner of Contented Corners. The humans watched in amazement, the bikers dismounting their rides in stunned silence.

"THAT'S IT. LET'S GET YOU HOME NOW. IT'S TIME FOR SOUP."

When the beasts had made it over to John, he handed the bullhorn off to Devon, who was at his side. He walked up and began to pet his beloved animals. Small flames shot out of Mewati's nostrils. Acid dripped from the side udders of Lactose Tolerant. The three calves panted and snarled, drooling madly, yet somehow happily. Beefy, John Steerman's favorite farm animal, began to purr.

The peaceful gathering was interrupted by the sound of a car horn blaring out a loud "AHOOOGA."

Around the corner from the north side of the arena, the giant Cattle-ac, driven by Red Simford, slowly turned. Dutch Friesian was laid out flat across the hood of the vehicle, holding on to the giant horns. Red sounded the klaxon once again.

"AHOOOGA."

Apparently, the best plan Red could come up with was to drive headlong at steamroller speed into the middle of the conflict, hoping that the cowsters would think a metallic giant steer was in their midst, thereby creating the mother of all distractions. Given recent developments, the snail-paced interruption didn't quite have the desired effect.

Red thought about chastising The Henchman for his failure to yell out a sequence of moos as they'd planned, but once he saw that the bizarre creatures appeared to be under control, he turned off the Cattle-ac's engine and climbed out, walking toward the others. He left Dutch to struggle with the massive horns up on the hood of the vehicle. It was then that, as if out of nowhere, the spinning, inverted tornado that Red and Dutch had seen the previous afternoon appeared once again, this time directly overhead. Everyone, both human and mutated cattle, looked up in unison at the twisting dunce cap-shaped cloud. It descended to about a hundred feet over the Cow Palace parking lot, right above them all.

Dutch Friesian, still laid out atop the car hood, thought to himself, *"Now THAT is a distraction!"*

🐂🐂🐂

Crewmember One thought this would be easier. All they needed to do was fire off the beacon to the pre-established coordinates, meet the intelligent cow-like creature there, transport him or her up to the ship and head back home. He never considered the fact that more than one bovine would show up to the landing site.

"This place is lousy with cows," observed Crewmember Two.

From their vantage point, a hundred feet above the Cow Palace and descending, looking out from their observation window, it was impossible to tell which of the beings below was the one they were seeking.

"Is there no way to make out which beast is the smart beast?" asked Crewmember One.

"I am afraid not," replied Crewmember Two. "From up here, they all look alike. I can tell the difference between the beasts that are similar to us and the two-legged species, but our instruments just can't get more precise than that. What are we going to do?"

"Drop down lower," instructed Crewmember One.

Beefy and the cows on the ground appeared as absorbed by the twister as the humans, and all were gazing up at the spinning dunce cap. The inverted vortex descended and was now level with the top of the arena. The base of the dunce cap was directly overhead both man and animal, and flashing colored lights and streaks of metal became visible through the twisting, swirling brown clouds that covered the entire cone.

Crewmember Two provided the disappointing update. "Sorry, it's not helping. At this level, there is all manner of planetary interference with the instruments. I just can't be certain which creature is which. Should we just go ahead and land?"

"No, they may not be as stupid as they look," replied Crewmember One. Then, after some consideration, he threw up his hooves and said, "Ah, moo it. We'll take them all back with us. Pull all of them up. At least the ones who look like us."

"You got it," replied Crewmember Two, thrusting several levers forward in a complicated sequence.

At once, all of the swirling clouds that were imbedded in the surface of the spaceship dissipated, and the folks and animals on the ground were left looking up at a bona fide spaceship. It resembled a really tall, really narrow pyramid. It made no noise whatsoever, and for a bit just hovered over the parking lot.

"I knew it!" said an excited Red Simford. "It's the government!"

Everyone else, Beefy included, figured the dunce cap-shaped spaceship was exactly that: a dunce cap-shaped spaceship.

And then, a series of spotlights went on, all at once, shining directly on some of the beings in the parking lot, but not others. The light seemed to freeze those it landed upon, and in a stunned, motionless state, they started to rise up into the air, being pulled up toward the alien spacecraft.

The three little cows, Huey, Crackle and Curly, rose up first. They didn't look frightened or disturbed in any way, just frozen in time as they were pulled upward. Next went Lactose Tolerant, a goofy and yet serene expression on her face.

"They're taking the cows," observed Han, giving Shorty a slight nudge.

He wasn't entirely correct, as next up went Brad, the cow mascot.

"I told you that guy was good," The Henchman said to no one in particular.

The last to be taken was Beefy, the one the extraterrestrials had come for in the first place.

John Steerman, resigned to the fact that there wasn't much he could do to stop the proceedings, especially since he'd left his lasso back in the pickup with the aardvarks, tipped his imaginary hat toward the bull. "Beefmaster," was all the farmer said.

Devon put his arm around his father's shoulder. "Bye, Beefy!" he cried.

And with that, the lights went out and the surface of the spaceship began to swirl once again. As silently as it had descended, the craft started to rise into the air.

"What about her?" called out Salers Salorn, pointing over to Mewati. Apparently, from above, the dragon-cow looked more like a dragon than a cow. Now it appeared as though the fire-breather would be left behind.

Gazing up mournfully, Mewati let out an extended, purposeful moo. Then, to everyone's amazement, wings emerged from the animal's sides. A few flaps of the furry appendages and up Mewati lifted. The dragon-cow could fly!

"Wow!" uttered a stunned Devon.

His father was clearly amazed as well, and added, "Yep."

Straight up Mewati climbed, and after a few seconds it looked like the cow was absorbed into the bottom of the dunce cap. A short while after that, the spaceship zoomed vertically to about a half a mile high, hovered there for a bit and then shot west toward the ocean, directly over the top of Bay City. It left in its wake a vapor trail the likes of which had never been seen. A magnificent triple rainbow lingered above the wounded metropolis; a tri-prism of hope, and the promise of better days to come.

🐂 🐂 🐂

It took some time for Contented Corners to get back to normal. John never did replace the cows, but didn't seem to mind that much, as it afforded him more time to spend with the aardvarks and his whittling. Caceres was as dedicated and talented as ever, and once his fabulous flowers, aided in blooming by an entirely new custom fertilizer, hit their full glorious radiance, the farm again became a destination. It was a place city folks or travelers on Highway One could stop for a spell and be transported back to a simpler time. Margaret O'Leary still graced the grounds with her presence, and it seemed that she and Dr. Herens were developing quite the romance. She'd potty-trained Chicken One and was working on trying to teach the bird how to fetch and roll over. Again, a harkening back to days of yore.

Officer Holstein resumed his beat back up on Lineback Street. The polite policeman's mere presence brought normalcy back to the area, so damaged after the night of the storm. Holstein would bow and smile, and bow again. His kindness and encouraging spirit were infectious. Within a few short months, Lineback Street was back in business. In fact, Ivory Chateaubriand even opened up her own little store near the Estonian Native Muumuu Shop. Called Shades of Ivory, the charming establishment sold, appropriately enough, sunglasses.

It took longer, several years, to rebuild Fishyman's Wharf, but eventually civilization returned to the area, albeit behind a new and impressive sea wall. Eventually, the Bay City spirit was back on E.I., and new and exciting shops, tourist destinations and a spectacular new Bay City Police Department precinct building were constructed. Once again, Fishyman's Wharf became world famous.

Down the road a bit in the Financial District, things were back to normal in a few days. The damage here, caused not by the storm but by the rampaging mutants, was enormous. Acid-melted and burned-out storefronts, piles of demolished vehicles and hundreds of shattered windows littered the area. But, the money people couldn't afford to be without their money-based hub of operations for any significant length of time. After some influential money people contacted influential political people, the National Army Engineering Corps was brought in and the area was rebuilt in almost no time at all. By mid-week it was as though the mutated cattle carnage had never occurred.

Red, Dutch and most of the bikers returned back to their pre-storm lives. Red gave up on his obsession with being the top Tauros dealer in the nation and Dutch continued to develop new and unique tea blends, which he'd offer up to prospective car buyers at Simford Auto Sales. The bullfighter and impressionist were hired by Red and performed daily at the car lot, though truth be told most shoppers had no clue what either of them had to do with buying a car.

Kenana's wounds, which were primarily internal, were completely healed by her immersion in the salt water. And, as it turned out, the massive beast was every bit as much in love with the ocean as was Mrs. Beefy. The elephant-cow was amazingly buoyant and preferred acting as a huge surfboard, as opposed to doing the actual surfing. Both cows were accepted and adopted with great enthusiasm and glee by the surfing community, particularly the juvenile surfers, who in some cases were the grandchildren of longtime residents of the Bluffs. While the smaller Mrs. Beefy perfected her mad cow skills under the expert tutelage of Aliab, Kenana and Dingo teamed up and gave free surfing lessons to any child who wanted them – with parental approval of course. Dingo would assist the youngsters in climbing up on Kenana's back and have them squat wide and low like an expert surfer. The massive cow could hold six or seven kids at once. Kenana would activate her adhesion field, and the children would be held fast in proper surfing position. Then the giant cow would ride the waves, mooing happily amidst the oohs and aahs of the delighted children. After several good rides, and once Dingo was convinced progress for the session had been adequate, Kenana would reverse the adhesion field, launching the kids up and away from her body. They'd splash down into the water and bob back up in hysterics, laughing and asking for the cow to do it again. More often than not, sweet Kenana would oblige.

Bay City did, eventually, return to the grandeur of its pre-Bessie days. Odd tales and myths about the storm eventually replaced the facts, as is usually the case. Some folks claimed to have seen a gigantic sea serpent in the midst of the chaotic storm, others say a dragon tore down a clifftop restaurant. Still others say the Bay City Zoo walls were ripped open by the storm, and rabid rhinoceri rampaged through the city.

Just a handful of people know the truth, and only a few of them know the whole story. Bessie was no ordinary Northern Pacific mega-storm. It was no hurricane, and certainly was not a cyclone. The fact is, even calling Bessie a typhoon isn't quite accurate. The storm was the first, and luckily the only of its kind.

It was a Cowphoon.

ANTILOGUE

MISHIMA'S BICYCLE REPAIR WAS A fixture in the small fishing community of Gudali. The kindly Dr. Mishima, it seemed, could fix just about any type of bicycle. He was kind and generous and did good work at a low price. Dr. Mishima was well liked by one and all.

And yet he also harbored a great secret.

One Tuesday he was deep in concentration, working on rebuilding a sprocket for a Tauros seven-speed sand bike, when he was approached by his trusted employee, Matt Susaka. Matt typically manned the front of the shop and dealt with the customers, taking orders and ringing up sales. Mishima couldn't tell if the issue that brought the worker to the back of the store was urgent or not, as his associate usually played things close to the vest. His typically expressionless face was tough to read.

"Matt-san, what is it? How can I help you?" asked Dr. Mishima.

"I don't think I need any help, Dr. Ron," the associate replied.

"Please, call me Dr. Mishima," requested the bicycle repair expert. "Is there something that you need?"

"I don't think so," answered the young man.

Dr. Mishima shook his head. "In that case, could you please hand me that large screwdriver on the workbench? I need to pop off this sprocket."

"Sure," Matt-san said.

He walked a few steps over to the nearby workbench, looked things over and brought a blowtorch back to his mentor.

"No, Matt-san," Mishima began, then shrugged and said, "Oh, never mind." He grabbed the needed screwdriver off the center of the workbench and returned to the bicycle sprocket.

"Oh, I almost forgot to tell you," said Susaka. "It's all over the radio. We are supposed to lock everything up and do something called 'shelter in place.'"

That would have been good information to have had right off the bat.

"What?" asked Dr. Mishima. "Tell me Matt-san, and think hard. Why are we supposed to shelter in place?"

"Because of the chinchillas, sir," Matt-san answered.

"Matt-san, what chinchillas? What is going on?" asked the shop owner, rather urgently now.

"The giant mutant chinchillas that are headed this way," explained the assistant.

Within twenty minutes, Dr. Yan Mishima and Matt Susaka were on the main highway that led north out of the village. They didn't bother locking up the bicycle shop. Dr. Mishima doubted they'd be returning. The appearance of mutant chinchillas could mean only one thing, and, without hesitation, the scientific duo sped toward a secret laboratory very few people knew existed. Their destination was clear, despite the unlikeliness of it all.

They were headed back. Back to Wagyu Island.

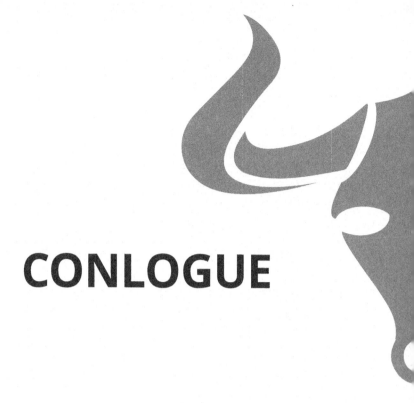

CONLOGUE

THE BESPECTACLED BEEFY ADDRESSED HIS fellow senators.

"My friends, much has transpired in the past several months, for me personally as well as for this planetoid I now call home. We stand at a crossroads, the barn door, if you will, of our future. Our home can support us no longer, and soon we shall depart en masse for my home planet. The question we must ask ourselves is, do we head to this new world as conquerors or as guests? Think carefully on your answer."

Mooing and mumbling rippled through the gathered throng. It was General Jutland who spoke up. Breaking traditional political protocol, the massive-headed cow-alien stepped up to the speaker's platform.

"The real question here, my friends, is this: What would you rather eat? What do you prefer your children eat? Fresh green grass, or hay?"

A dissatisfied moo echoed throughout the chambers. The consensus was unanimous. The cow-beings hated hay.

General Jutland seized the opportunity. "The choice is clear. We must activate the war cannons. We have them ready to mount onto the starships. There's no sense in leaving them here anyway."

A clapping of hooves began to ring out. Beefy was losing his argument and losing control of this crowd. The general shoved him aside and took over the podium.

"Those who are not with us are against us!" he charged. "We shall seize this new world and make it ours! No off-worlder can decide our future, only destiny can do that. And destiny has spoken!"

Wild clapping, mooing and stomping broke out. The crowd had become a mob and left unchecked would begin to stampede.

Beefy snuck down a back passageway where he was greeted by Brad, the former mascot. Brad was wearing an impressive black and white spotted cow costume made from curtains and was holding his cow head under his right arm.

"That turned ugly fast," Brad said to Beefy.

"You're telling me. Is the shuttle pod ready?" the bull asked.

"Gassed up and ready to go," answered Brad. "All provisions are on board. In short order we'll be back on Earth."

"Well then, there's no point in sticking around here. Let's go. We've got to warn an entire planet."

And down the passageway the friends headed, all of humankind's future resting in the palms of their hooves.

B ACK IN THE DAY, GLEN Granholm was editor-in-chief of the Meadows Elementary School mimeographed magazine. Later, he worked as a skateboarding political reporter for the Daily Nexus newspaper at the University of California at Santa Barbara.

Even later, he published two books based on the locally semi-popular Great Roseburg Trivia Challenge, held annually in southern Oregon for more than twenty years. *You Gotta Be Kidding! The Ultimate Trivia Quizbook,* and its follow-up, *You REALLY Gotta Be Kidding! More of the Ultimate Trivia Quizbook* are hard to find, but fun to read and play.

Then Glen wrote "Experience, Strength and Hope: A Love Story". This work got some wonderful reviews.

Cowphoon is Glen's first work of fiction. More mutant and weather stories are on the way.

Glen lives in Southern California with his wife Trish, Aunt Ival, Connie and several animals.